The Hasidic Masters' Guide to Management

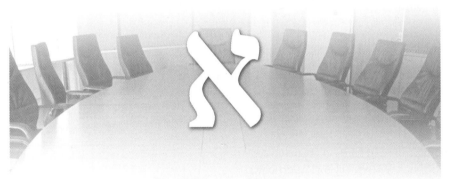

By Moshe Kranc

Edited by Fern Levitt

I dedicate this book to my father, Sam Kranc of blessed memory.

He loved to tell a good story, and his life was itself quite a story.

TABLE OF CONTENTS

ACKNOWLEDGEMENTS

I would like to thank –

My wife Elise for her encouragement, support and feedback throughout this project.

My children Aaron, Hannan, Tehilla, Jacob, David and Noam for letting me use the computer.

My mother Sara, who taught me the values I write about in this book.

My sister Lisa, for her frank and supportive feedback gleaned from her extensive management experience.

My mentors, Rabbi Yankel Kranz and Ariella Deem Goldberg, who taught me to enjoy the tension between the secular and the holy.

Yossi Tsuria, *il migliore fabbro.*

Bill DeKeyser, who helped me crystallize a vague desire to write stories into the book you see before you.

My editor, Fern Levitt, for helping me articulate the ideas in this book.

Jeff Herman, Tom Miller, Matin Rutte, Yaacov Peterseil and Stephen Kurer, for their invaluable feedback at critical phases of this undertaking.

Managers who have taught me by their (mostly good) example: Ara Avakian, Jit Saxena, Bob O'Donaghue, Paul Dale, Shimshon Kaufman, Abe Peled, Raffi Kesten, Bob Rosenschein, Daniel Schreiber, Ofer Yuval.

I echo Martin Buber's introduction to his *Tales of the Hasidim:* "Along with much else, I owe this composition to the air of this land. Our sages say it makes one wise; to me it has granted a different gift: the strength to make a new beginning."

The disciples of Rabbi Menachem Mendel of Kotsk once asked him why he did not write a book. He replied, "Let's suppose that I took the trouble to write a book. My opponents would not buy it, for they despise me. So, only my followers would purchase the book. Now, our people are poor, and work hard during the week, so they will only have time to read my book on the Sabbath. And when will they get to it on the Sabbath? After they have prayed the Friday evening service, and enjoyed a festive meal with their families – only then will they have time to read. So, let's suppose one of my followers stretches out on his sofa, takes the book and opens it. He is tired from the week's work and drowsy from the meal, and he quickly falls asleep, the book slipping from his hand to the floor. Now, tell me, shall I go to the trouble of writing a book just to put my followers to sleep?"

"It was only when I wrote my first book that the world I wanted to live in opened to me."[1]

- Anaïs Nin

INTRODUCTION

The first time I used a traditional Jewish story in a business setting was at my company's annual strategy conference, where I was asked to present the new technologies we were developing in our labs. As I looked out at my fellow managers who had gathered in Seville, Spain from our corporate offices all over the globe, I knew that research was the last thing on their minds. The company had recently gone public, and the stock that had been issued at $20 was rapidly approaching $100. My colleagues wanted to hear about products that could keep investor momentum going, not high-risk inventions that, if they panned out, would take years to come to market.

I decided to try an unconventional approach. "I've come to Spain from our Israeli office, so I'd like to begin with a Jewish Spanish story. Almost one thousand years ago, in Moslem Spain, there lived a Jew named Rabbi Samuel the Prince. He was very wise, and rose to great power, becoming the Sultan's treasurer. This aroused the jealousy of the other ministers, who planted rumors that Rabbi Samuel was embezzling money from the royal treasury.

The Sultan decided to put Rabbi Samuel to the test. One day, without warning, he called for Rabbi Samuel, and asked him to make a complete accounting of his personal wealth. Rabbi Samuel was taken aback, but he could not refuse the Sultan's request. He sat at a table, asked for a quill and parchment, and began writing feverishly. After half an hour, he stopped, reviewed the list silently, and handed it to the Sultan.

The Sultan read the inventory carefully, and slammed it down angrily on the table. 'Why, this is only a fraction of your wealth. I personally have given you far more than what you list here as your salary. This is a brazen lie! My advisors are correct – you have been dishonest with me in your monetary affairs. I shall personally confiscate everything you own. Guards, take this man away!'

'Your Majesty', responded Rabbi Samuel, 'you asked me for an accounting of my wealth. As you can plainly see, my worldly possessions are not truly mine. At any time, they could be taken from me by robbers, war or natural disaster. In fact, your Majesty has just taken them from me with a single command.'

'The only possession I truly own is that money which can never be taken from me – the money I have given to charity. You see, a Jew is commanded by the Torah to give one tenth of his income to those in need. The figure I gave you, your Majesty, was the total of all the moneys I have given to charity. That is my true wealth, for the benefit from that money remains mine forever, and can never be taken from me.'

The Sultan was impressed by this profound truth, and promoted Rabbi Samuel to even greater power in his kingdom."

I paused for a moment and looked around at my attentive audience. "Rabbi Samuel has hit upon a fundamental aspect of human nature – we are easily confused between what is truly ours and what others grant us. The same is true of corporations. Our stock price is soaring, but that is something that is granted by investors, and could be taken away from us tomorrow by those very same investors, based on factors that are entirely out of our control. What, then, is truly ours? It's our loyal, highly skilled employees, and the passion and innovation that they bring to their jobs. They are our true strategic assets, and they are what will keep us successful for years to come. I'd like to present to you some of the new product ideas they've come up with."

From the contemplative faces of my fellow managers, I could see that my unorthodox introduction had succeeded. It wasn't me who had convinced them that the subject was important – they had convinced themselves, by internalizing a story steeped in tradition and wisdom.

Since then, I've used traditional Jewish stories, especially Hasidic tales, in a variety of management contexts: to motivate teams, to impart a lesson to a fellow manager, to grab an audience's attention. Almost always, I've found that the message gets across. Why Hasidic stories? Because the Hasidic tale has a world of timeless insight and wisdom for the modern business world. The Hasidic Masters were exceedingly wise leaders who understood the human heart. They used stories as a medium to transmit values and stimulate insights on the part of their followers. By emphasizing the human perspective, Hasidism transformed and enriched the Jewish establishment of its time. We cannot speak with the Masters directly about management issues, but the insights of the

Hasidic perspective can provide important lessons for today's business world.

Hasidism is a Jewish mystical movement founded in the 18th century by Rabbi Israel, the *Ba'al Shem Tov* (Master of the Good Name). This revolutionary movement emerged in response to the crises of its time, in the aftermath of the Cossack massacres and mass disillusionment with false Messiahs. Some rabbis of the era suspected Hasidism of being yet another dangerous messianic movement and went to great lengths to oppose its spread.

The genius of Hasidism, and the secret of its success, lay in its ability to supplement rather than subvert Rabbinic Judaism. Hasidism did not negate the values of the rabbinic establishment – but it equally emphasized other values. It recognized the tension between the letter and the spirit of Jewish law, and looked for a balance that gave legitimacy to the ethical intent of legislation, even when this required bending the letter of the law. It was anti-elitist, valuing sincerity and devotion over erudition or wealth. The poor and unlearned Jew became a heroic figure who could move the heavens with prayer. It established the role of the *Tzaddik* (righteous one) or *Rebbe* (master) to provide inspiration and guidance in both spiritual and worldly matters. It employed the powerful means of stories, parables, and anecdotes to transmit wisdom. Hasidism succeeded where other Jewish sects failed because it was an evolutionary as well as a revolutionary movement.

There are striking parallels between the circumstances that catalyzed the Hasidic revolution and the world of business today. In modern business, the inherent tension between the "letter of the law" and the "spirit of the law" expresses itself in choosing between maximum shareholder profits, even if only temporarily and on paper, and ethical behavior; Hasidism looks for a balance that respects both. Today's employees are all too often frustrated by their inability to act on their personal values and beliefs in the workplace. The Rabbis who led the Jewish mystical movement were not mystics in the most common sense of the word – they did not seek to leave this world to dwell in another. Rather, they were what Rabbinic scholar Max Kadushin refers to as "normal mystics", who sought to integrate the Divine into even the most mundane day-to-day activities of this world.

With each new corporate scandal, the public has grown increasingly hostile towards senior managers; Hasidism sought to narrow a similar

11

schism by elevating the value of the common man. Today's senior managers aspire to provide inspirational leadership that can give employees a vision of where they are going and why they want to get there; Hasidism provides us with vivid examples of such leadership. Rather than advocating a humanistic revolution in management, Hasidism teaches that new people-oriented values can successfully be fused with existing business practices in an evolutionary process.

My goal in writing this book is to share with you some of my favorite stories, from Hasidic and other traditional Jewish sources, stories that have important leadership lessons for the modern business world. I have organized the tales in this book according to the management functions suggested by Peter Drucker in his classic analysis *Management: Tasks, Responsibilities, Practices*[2]: motivating and communicating, setting objectives, organizing the group, measuring performance, developing people, and managing the outside world. The tales in this book provide insight into each of these roles of management. I have also included modern business examples of the principles illuminated by the stories. I do not presume to call this a comprehensive management program, but I hope you will find the stories thought-provoking, especially about your own management style. To share your own comments and feedback with me, please visit *The Hasidic Masters' Guide to Management* on the Web at www.hasidicmanagement.com.

There is a well-established genre of business books that looks for wisdom from eclectic sources. So, though you may have already studied management at the feet of other masters – learned the art of war from Sun Tzu[3], gleaned leadership secrets from Attila the Hun[4], and admired the strategic insights of Machiavelli's Prince[5] – I invite you to savor and be inspired by the management wisdom of the Hasidic Rabbis.

Rabbi Jacob Kranc (pronounced *Krantz*), a well-known teller of Jewish fables known as the *Magid* (Preacher) of Dubno, was my distinguished ancestor, so perhaps story-telling is an inherited family occupation. In honor of the 200th anniversary of the passing of the Dubno Magid, and to mark my own 50th jubilee year, I have written this book to share with you the business world in which I want to live, a world inhabited by enlightened, humanistic managers.

MOSHE KRANC
JERUSALEM, SPRING 2004

12

CHAPTER 1

Motivating and Communicating

Dilbert, November 22, 2003

Rabbi Israel Salanter, the Chief Rabbi of Jerusalem, once sat with his fellow rabbis discussing their congregations. Rabbi Israel listened as the other rabbis told of struggles with their rebellious and unruly flocks.

"I have no such problem," he volunteered. "I have full confidence that my congregation will follow any command I give."

The other rabbis looked at him quizzically. "What is the source of your confidence?" they asked.

"It is simple," answered Rabbi Israel with a smile. "I never give my congregation any command I do not think they will follow."

"...a manager *motivates and communicates*. He makes a team out of the people that are responsible for various jobs. He does that through the practices with which he manages. He does it in his own relation to the men he manages. He does it through incentives and rewards for successful work. He does it through his promotion policy. And he does it through constant communication, both from the manager to his subordinate, and from the subordinate to the manager."[6]

- Peter F. Drucker

אТhe Hasidic Rebbe seeks to ignite the spark that lies dormant in his followers. They must be motivated to work together in order to overcome mundane distractions and achieve ever more challenging spiritual goals. The Rebbe's success in motivating appears effortless, for he only asks from his followers what they themselves already want to give.

The Rebbe generally does not rely on direct commands to make his point. He communicates indirectly, via illustrations, by telling stories, and leading by example through his actions. He not only preaches, but lives, his values.

Let's examine how the Hasidic Masters interact with their followers: motivating people and communicating with the team.

MOTIVATING

Lesson 1: Be Willing To Take The First Penny

Taking the First Coin

One evening the students of Rabbi Dov Baer, the Preacher of Mezritch, were sitting in the study hall. Each of them – Shneur Zalman of Liadi, Levi Yitzhak of Berditchev and Elimelekh of Lizhensk – would later found a great Hasidic dynasty, but in those days they were still young students.

Their discussion was interrupted when the caretaker rushed in shouting, "Kidnappers! Kidnappers! They've taken Yosef Isaacs!" He spotted the students and ran to them.

"His life is in danger! The kidnappers demand a ransom of 600 gold coins by dawn or they will kill him! We must find a way to save Yosef Isaacs!"

"600 gold coins!" exclaimed Levi Yitzchak. "How could we possibly raise that much money? Even if every Jew in Mezritch donated all his worldly possessions, it would still not come to 600 gold coins. All we can do is pray to God that Yosef Isaacs is delivered from the kidnappers' hands."

"There is a way to raise 600 gold coins," said Shneur Zalman thoughtfully. "There is one Jew in town who has that much money. Have you forgotten Velvel the Apostate?"

"Velvel?" snorted Elimelekh. "He left the Jewish people years ago. He even lives among the Gentile princes outside of town! His hatred of anything Jewish runs so deep that whenever a Jew approaches his palace he sends his pack of dogs to tear him limb from limb!"

"Even so," said Shneur Zalman, "he is our only hope, for only he has enough money to pay such a ransom. I intend to go and ask him to help save his fellow Jew."

Seeing Shneur Zalman's determination, his friends insisted on accompanying him to protect him from harm.

"You may join me," said Shneur Zalman, "but on one condition – you must both remain silent, and let me alone speak with Velvel." They agreed and set off together.

Miraculously, they arrived at Velvel's home without encountering any guard dogs, and knocked on the door. Velvel himself opened it. He was taken aback by the sight of the three Hasidic students.

"I see the Jews have forgotten how much I despise their visits," he said. "I shall have to get more dogs!"

"Please, hear me out," said Shneur Zalman. "We've come on an urgent mission." Shneur Zalman explained the purpose of their visit – how Yosef Isaacs' life hung in the balance, what a tragedy it would be for Yosef Isaacs' wife and children if he were killed, the great reward that awaited any Jew who participated in the redemption of captives, and how the ransom was more than the Jewish community of Mezritch could raise without Velvel's help.

Velvel was moved. "You've shown great courage in coming here," he said. "Many years ago, I put something aside to donate to a worthy cause. I believe this is the occasion to give it. Wait here and I will bring it to you." Shneur Zalman looked at his surprised friends triumphantly.

Velvel returned and, with a flourish, he handed Shneur Zalman – a single penny!

"There you are, young man," he said. "I wish you luck in raising the rest of the ransom."

Levi Yitzhak and Elimelekh were about to rebuke Velvel for his miserliness. One penny, indeed! But Shneur Zalman silenced them with a look.

"Thank you so much," said Shneur Zalman to Velvel. "I appreciate your effort to assist in our cause. May God reward you for your part in saving a fellow Jew's life." There was no irony in Shneur Zalman's voice, only sincere gratitude. With that, Shneur Zalman turned to leave, with his stunned companions following him.

They had taken only a few steps when they heard Velvel's voice behind them.

"Wait! Perhaps I can find something else in the house to contribute." They returned to the door, and Velvel reappeared after a few minutes to give them – two pennies! Again, Shneur Zalman was effusive in his thanks, and they turned to leave.

Velvel called them back a third time, and gave them ten pennies; the fourth time, a gold coin; the fifth time, five gold coins. Each time, Shneur Zalman was genuinely thankful, without a hint of reproof in his voice. They did not leave Velvel that night until he had donated the entire amount needed to rescue the captive – 600 gold coins.

As they walked back to town, Elimelekh asked in admiration, "How did you know that our mission to Velvel would be successful?"

"I knew that Velvel had within him the strength to give the entire sum, if only he could give the first penny," said Shneur Zalman. "His problem was that no one was willing to take the first penny from him. Once

I took it with sincere gratitude and encouragement, the wellsprings of his soul were opened up and he was able to give the entire amount."

To Bring Out The Best In People, Expect The Best, But Be Willing To Take The First Penny

Shneur Zalman transforms Velvel because he believes that Velvel is capable of great deeds, and he understands the symbolic value of the first penny. This is the work of management in a nutshell: to take the first penny, what people think they can give, and then challenge them to meet ever higher expectations.

Think about the best manager you ever had. Was it someone who set low expectations and assigned you modest tasks that could be accomplished with reasonable effort? Probably not. That kind of manager doesn't promote growth or stick in people's minds. Or did your most memorable manager set high expectations, challenge you to do something ambitious, and give you the guidance that enabled you to succeed? Are you as a manager providing ambitious but achievable expectations, challenges and a sense of accomplishment to your team?

In Today's World

In his article "Pygmalion in Management"[7], J. Sterling Livingston proves that subordinates' performance rises or falls to meet managers' expectations. If managers' expectations are high, productivity is likely to be excellent, while if their expectations are low, productivity is likely to be poor.

Livingston cites a number of experiments that prove this point. For example, at Metropolitan Life Insurance, salesmen were divided into a "superstaff" of high achievers and an "average" unit of salesmen who were considered merely adequate. The superstaff consistently exceeded sales goals, while the performance of salesmen in the average unit actually declined. Perhaps the superstaff's improvement was due to their innate talent. The average salesmen's performance decline can only be attributed to the decreased expectations from their superiors.

Another study of managers, this one at AT&T, demonstrated that their relative success, as measured by salary increases and promotions, depended largely on the company's expectations.[8]

As Eliza Doolittle says in George Bernard Shaw's Pygmalion, "The difference between a lady and a flower girl is not how she behaves but how she's treated."

א

In my first performance review as a manager of Quality Assurance, I was proud to report to my boss that all the major bugs in the products that had shipped that year had been discovered in my lab rather than in the field.

To my surprise, my manager viewed my year very differently. He gave no sign of appreciation, but he was prolific in pointing out ways in which I had failed. "You didn't build tools to speed up the testing process; you didn't provide guidance to Engineering as to how they could reduce the number of bugs; you didn't improve the method for tracking customer-discovered bugs." I was flabbergasted. In one moment, my entire view of the year was turned upside down – I had been playing defense when I should have been playing offense!

Obviously my manager should have told me sooner what he expected of me. And I would have liked to hear some positive feedback – he could have accepted my first penny more graciously. But, he did most emphatically ask me for the next penny, and the challenge spurred me on to accomplish things I didn't know I was capable of achieving.

Lesson 2: Provide Small Rewards Along The Way

Great Abundance

Rabbi Jacob Kranc, the Magid of Dubno, once delivered a sermon on God's promise to Abraham that his descendants would be enslaved for 400 years, "And then they shall go forth with great abundance" (Genesis 15:14).

When the Hebrews left Egypt, the Bible tells us that the Egyptians gave them "jewels of silver and gold, and raiment" (Exodus 12:35).

"Were these baubles of jewels and raiment the great wealth which God promised to Abraham?" Rabbi Jacob asked. "If so, Abraham should have declined both the slavery and the reward!"

In answer, he related a parable.

A father once apprenticed his son to a wealthy merchant for two years. The merchant was pleased with the boy, and when the apprenticeship was over, rewarded him handsomely with a hundred-ruble note.

To his surprise, the boy was crestfallen. He took the bill without comment and stuffed it into his pocket, then set out for home.

The next day, the boy's father came to see the merchant.

"I want to thank you," he said, "for your generosity to my son. But the boy does not understand the value of paper money. He is accustomed to the allowance I give him in pennies; he was expecting you to give him a bulging bag of shiny coins. Imagine his disappointment when he saw his two years of work reduced to a slip of paper!"

"I would be grateful if you could pay him part of his salary in coins," said the father. "He will appreciate the note when he is older and wiser. For now, he needs his wages in a form that even a young boy can enjoy."

So it was with the Jewish people after hundreds of years of slavery in Egypt, explained Rabbi Jacob. The "great abundance" which God promised Abraham refers to the giving of the Ten Commandments at Mount Sinai. Abraham himself understood the importance of this great gift to mankind.

But the Jewish slaves leaving Egypt could not appreciate such a subtle gift. God granted them, in addition, the kind of wealth they then valued – the gold, silver and raiment of the Egyptians.

Later, as the Children of Israel grew in wisdom, they came to understand that true wealth lies not in the sort of trinkets gathered in Egypt, but in the divine gift of God's law.

Reward The Team With Pennies On The Way To The Big Payoff

Rabbi Jacob has hit upon an important principle in motivating employees. Long-term incentives, such as stock options and revenue sharing plans, are important. Employees should know that their fortunes thrive together with the fortunes of the company.

However, these plans are too abstract to motivate employees to work hard from day to day. A manager must also provide concrete short-term rewards for extraordinary effort along the way to the big payoff. A team lunch, a certificate of appreciation, dinner-for-two after a month of overtime evenings – these direct, tangible rewards provide immediate motivation far more efficiently than any long-term company-wide incentive program.

In Today's World

In 1914, Ernest Shackleton led an expedition of 27 men in what was to be the first full crossing of Antarctica. His ship sank, marooning the crew. At many points over the months that followed it appeared that they were doomed. How did Shackleton manage to save the entire team and keep them from despair, knowing as they did that they should have been on a triumphal return to England rather than trapped on an ice floe?

Among his other management skills, Shackleton understood the importance of interim, tangible rewards to keep up motivation and morale. On December 5, 1915, the one-year anniversary of their departure, Shackleton held a holiday celebration to commemorate their triumph in having survived a full year.

The big payoff was when the crew finally arrived home – but the interim payoffs were what kept them going.[9]

During World War II, a pilot's plane was struck by anti-aircraft fire in the South Pacific. Somehow, despite the damage to the wings and engine, the pilot managed to coax the aircraft to carry him to safety.

At President Roosevelt's initiative, he and the pilot visited the Boeing plant where the plane had been built. The pilot thanked the workers for their attention to quality in the craft that had saved his life. Needless to say, the workers redoubled their efforts to produce the best possible airplane.[10]

Escalade Sports' President, Dan Messmer, found an original way to celebrate his sporting goods company's first $100 million year. A Brinks truck pulled up to the Evansville, Indiana corporate headquarters with $30,000 in cash, and Messmer personally handed each and every employee a crisp $100 note.[11]

Lesson 3: Be There With Your Team

Being There

Rabbi Abraham Jacob of Sadigora often told the following story about the founder of Hasidism, Rabbi Israel, the Ba'al Shem Tov:

One Friday afternoon, the Ba'al Shem Tov arrived unexpectedly at the synagogue in a remote village. The congregants were honored to have such a distinguished guest, and vied for the honor of hosting him for a Sabbath meal.

"I have no time for meals," said Rabbi Israel. "Jews are in grave danger, and we must pray for salvation."

After the Friday evening service, the Ba'al Shem Tov led the congregation in a fervent recitation of the Psalms and prayers. Several hours later, he allowed the townspeople to return briefly to their homes for a Sabbath meal, but later the congregation returned to the synagogue and recited Psalms through the night. At dawn, Rabbi Israel led the Sabbath morning prayers and read the weekly Torah portion.

As the morning service concluded, a look of relief passed over the Ba'al Shem Tov's face.

"Now I am ready to accept your offer of a Sabbath meal," he told one of the congregants. The entire community joined Rabbi Israel at the Sabbath table and listened to his words of Torah.

The meal was interrupted by a knock at the door. It was a Gentile peasant.

"Give me a shot of vodka," he said, "and I will tell you how you were saved last night."

Glass in hand, the peasant told his story. "Yesterday at dusk, the Lord Mayor assembled all the farmers in town, gave us guns, and told us to get ready to kill the Jews. All night we waited for the order to attack. At daybreak, a carriage drove up to the Lord Mayor's palace, and out stepped a distinguished gentleman. He went inside and spoke with the Lord Mayor. Then the Lord Mayor came outside and told us that we could all go home."

Rabbi Israel nodded and turned to the congregation.

"Your Lord Mayor has fallen upon hard times," he explained. "He has many silos full of grain from previous years' harvests that he has been unable to sell, and the grain will soon begin to rot. A trusted advisor convinced him that the Jews were conspiring to drive away buyers and bankrupt him. The Lord Mayor, in his rage, decided to kill all the Jews in town, and assembled the peasants for an attack."

"In order to save you, I brought the Lord Mayor's childhood friend back from the dead. The Lord Mayor does not yet know that his friend has died, and was happy to see him. When the Lord Mayor explained why the peasants were gathered outside, his friend told him, 'You are surely mistaken about the Jews. I do business with them regularly, and I have always found them to be honest and helpful. I suggest you contact them after their Sabbath, and ask them to help you sell your surplus wheat.' The Lord Mayor accepted his friend's advice, and ordered the peasants to disperse peacefully."

Rabbi Abraham Jacob of Sadigora continued, "At first glance, it seems odd that our Master the Ba'al Shem Tov had to travel all the way to a remote town in order to save it. Couldn't he have remained at home and worked his wonders from afar? Of course he could have! But he reasoned, 'If I succeed in my mission, then all is well. And if I do not succeed, then I want to be there, together with those people in their hour of distress.'"

In Times Of Stress, Be There With Your People

The Ba'al Shem Tov cultivated a hands-on leadership style. He could have stayed home, but he chose to be with his people, to share with them the hard work and the risk.

Managers sometimes have to lead their teams in an all-out effort to meet some company goal. It helps to be there with the team through all the extra hours, rather than managing by remote control. You may even find that you actually enjoy the intensity of a project under pressure, the sense of camaraderie and esprit-de-corps that unites the group. *'If I succeed in my mission, then all is well.'* – Your own personal example increases the team's energy level. *'And, if I do not succeed, then I want to be there, together with those people in their hour of distress.'* – The team needs to know that their effort is noticed and appreciated, and that you haven't asked them to do anything you're not willing to do yourself.

Who knows? When you roll up your sleeves, you may find a way to increase the project's chances of success through your own contribution.

In Today's World

The Israeli Army, recognized as one of the most effective fighting forces in the world, is built upon the principle of personal example. An officer is always expected to personally lead his troops in battle.

The fact that senior officers take front-line combat positions means that Israel suffers the highest rate of officer-to-soldier casualties in the world. However, the Israeli Army believes that leading by example increases respect for officers and instills greater motivation among soldiers.

Dick Vermeil, the coach of the St. Louis Rams, kept a wheelbarrow on the sidelines during the entire season of his team's remarkable run to the Super Bowl championship in 2000. When asked why, he told this story:

A man who came to a small town declared that one week hence he would push a wheelbarrow across a high-wire spanning the nearby canyon. Everyone scoffed except a farmer who went to the edge of town to watch the daredevil practice crossing a wire stretched five feet off the ground.

"I've seen him and I believe he can do it," the farmer told his friends, who jeered in reply. So the farmer said, "I'm so sure he can do it that I'll bet $20 with anyone who thinks he can't."

On the big day the farmer told the daredevil, "I know you can do it. I'm so sure that I even bet $20 with anyone who said otherwise."

The performer looked him in the eye and said, "That's not real belief. If you really believe, then get in the wheelbarrow!"[12]

Coach Vermeil's point was that it is easy to sit on the sidelines and pay lip service to the team's goals and the sacrifice required to achieve them. But if you really believe, then when the wheelbarrow comes out, everyone – the manager and every last member of the team – must climb in.

Lesson 4: The Outcome Is Entirely In Your Hands

The Unlocked Gate

The Talmud tells us that, in Heaven, the gates of salvation are never locked – they are always open to the prayers of the broken-hearted. Rabbi Simcha Bunim of P'shischa once asked his Hasidim, "If the gates are always open, then why did God put gates there? What purpose do they serve?"

He explained, "The gates keep out those who do not even try. Seeing the gates, some immediately assume that the way is barred, and they turn back. If only they would give the slightest push, God Himself would swing the gates open wide and clear the way before them."

It May Only Take The Smallest Push To Open A Gate You Assumed Was Locked

The Answer Is In Your Hands

In the Golden Age of the eleventh century, Spanish Jews participated fully in their country's financial and political affairs. The leader of the Jewish community, Rabbi Samuel the Prince, became the King's treasurer and trusted advisor.

His conspicuous success made him the target of constant attacks by disgruntled rivals within the King's inner circle. Rabbi Samuel relied on his wits to foil the plots against him.

Once the King's Royal Chancellor, Prince Carlos, devised a plan to discredit Rabbi Samuel.

"The King trusts Rabbi Samuel because the Jew always gives wise answers to the King's questions. If Rabbi Samuel cannot answer a question correctly, the King will see that he is as fallible as any other advisor." Carlos thought long and hard in order to concoct such a question.

One day Carlos presented the King with a particularly difficult financial dilemma.

"The problem is indeed puzzling," said the King. "I will ask Rabbi Samuel for his advice."

This was the opening Carlos had been waiting for.

"With all due respect, Your Majesty," he said, "it pains me to see how that Jew tricks you into believing that he is wise. He is no wiser than your other advisors. Why, I could ask him the simplest question and he would give the wrong answer."

The King was amused by this challenge.

"Carlos, you do not appreciate Rabbi Samuel's wisdom. I am sure that he can give the correct answer

30

to any question you pose to him. I invite you to join us this afternoon and put him to the test."

When Rabbi Samuel arrived to speak with the King, he was surprised to also see Prince Carlos.

"Hello, Rabbi Samuel," said the King. "Before we begin, the Royal Chancellor has a question to ask you."

"Rabbi Samuel," said Carlos, "I hear you are the wisest of men. Perhaps in your great wisdom you can tell me what I hold in my hands?"

Rabbi Samuel understood immediately that this was a test, one that he must not fail. Looking closely at Carlos' clasped hands, he discerned a tuft of white between two fingers. "You are holding a small bird," Rabbi Samuel said.

"That is correct, Rabbi Samuel," said Carlos, "but your answer is incomplete. Please tell me: is the bird in my hands alive or dead?"

Thought Carlos, "Now I have him. Whatever he says, he will be wrong. If he says the bird is dead, I will open my hands and show the King that the bird is, in fact, alive. If he says that the bird is alive, I will snap its neck as I open my fingers, and Rabbi Samuel will also be proven wrong."

The King waited expectantly as Rabbi Samuel looked at Carlos' hands. Samuel paused, lost in thought. When he spoke, he chose his words carefully.

"The answer," he said, "is in your hands."

"Well spoken!" exclaimed the King with pleasure. "Rabbi Samuel, you are indeed the wisest of men. And now, Carlos, please excuse us – Rabbi Samuel and I have important matters to discuss."

Your Fate Is Not Sealed –The Answer Is Entirely In Your Hands

R abbi Simcha tells us that God helps those who help themselves – the smallest push can cause the gates of salvation to swing wide open. In business, too, hard workers tend to benefit from lucky breaks and tail winds more often than do slackers. As the old adage has it, "Luck is the residue of hard work."

Carlos believes that he controls Rabbi Samuel's destiny, but by recognizing that the bird's fate has not yet been sealed, Rabbi Samuel is able to regain control of his own fate.

Is your team paralyzed by the enormity of the task ahead of them? Perhaps there are only two weeks left to accomplish five weeks worth of work, or perhaps a product cannot be delivered without first solving some last-minute technical conundrum. A team, like the proverbial deer in the headlights, may be paralyzed with anxiety, certain that the project is doomed to failure no matter what they do. Your job as manager is to convince each and every team member that the project's success or failure hangs on her individual effort, or in Rabbi Samuel's words, "The answer is in your hands."

Remember Henry Ford's dictum: "Whether you think you can or whether you think you can't, you're probably right."

Whatever the barrier, all you can ask of your team members is to give it their best shot. You'll be surprised at how often that is enough to overcome even the most intimidating obstacles.

In Today's World

Some companies base hiring decisions on the characteristics of initiative and aggressiveness. In their book *Hidden Value: How Great Companies Achieve Extraordinary Results with Ordinary People*[13], Charles O'Reilly and Jeffrey Pfeffer describe PSS World Medical, a specialty marketer and distributor of medical products to physicians.

Pat Kelly, CEO of PSS, gauges these attributes through his hiring strategy. He does not call back job applicants after the initial interview. Only candidates who themselves initiate the follow-up contact continue in the hiring process. PSS thus determines whether the candidate is entrepreneurial and aggressive enough to pursue the job on his own. This hiring strategy has built a top-performing sales force – as of 1999, PSS's five-year growth rate in sales revenue was 52% annually.

Determination, together with good breaks, can sometimes help you accomplish the near-impossible. This was the moral I gleaned from an experience I had years ago, which gave me the uncanny feeling that I was personally living a Hasidic tale.

I was working on a project that required a series of business trips to Los Angeles. As long as I was on the West Coast, I would sometimes spend the weekend with my in-laws Jason and Jane in Seattle. Once, when I was in Los Angeles on business, I learned that Jane's mother had passed away.

As an Orthodox Jew, I do not travel on the Sabbath, from sundown Friday to sundown Saturday. I wanted to fly to Seattle to pay my condolences to Jane, for it is an important *mitzva* (worthy deed) to console the bereaved during the first week of mourning. But my Friday agenda ended with a meeting that was due to run long beyond the scheduled departure of the last flight I could take to Seattle.

Still, on a hunch, I checked out of my hotel on Friday morning. "After all," I reasoned, "perhaps the meeting will end earlier than expected, and I might still have a chance to get to Seattle. If not, I'll have plenty of time to check back in later."

Lo and behold, the meeting was short and successful, and I found myself in a rented car forty-five minutes before the Seattle flight's departure. I knew that, with normal traffic, it would take an hour to get to the airport. But I wanted to expend every possible effort to get to Seattle. "In any case," I thought, "if I miss the plane, I'll have plenty of time to get back to my hotel before sundown."

Amazingly, the freeway to the airport was clear, and I reached the rental return office in a record thirty minutes. I ran into the office with the car keys and instructed the puzzled clerk, "If I don't come back within half an hour, process the return."

33

In the terminal, I discovered that there still was room on the flight and time enough to board. The flight's scheduled arrival time would allow me to get from the Seattle airport to Jane's house before sundown, with an hour to spare. So, much to my surprise, I found myself on an airplane headed to Seattle.

Now the bad news — our arrival in Seattle was delayed due to inclement weather. By the time the plane landed, only twenty minutes remained until sunset.

On my previous trip to Seattle a month earlier, my well-meaning Sikh taxi driver, Rajib, had gotten lost searching for Jane's home in the cul-de-sac streets near the university. What should have been a twenty-minute trip had turned into a forty-five minute ordeal.

Now, I dove into the first cab in the line at the taxi stand. Without looking up, I read Jane's address to the driver. "Please," I begged, "just tell me you know how to get there quickly."

"Certainly I do," came a familiar voice. "I took you there last month!"

I looked up to see the turban-framed beaming face of my old friend, Rajib. He got me to my destination in 15 minutes flat. I was able to offer my condolences and prepare for the Sabbath as well.

I know this was not strictly due to a miracle. But I like to think that I did my part by sparing no effort to perform a worthy deed. If God rewarded me by giving me a little extra help, I certainly am grateful.

COMMUNICATING

Lesson 5: A Story Can Redeem Both The Teller And The Listener

I Hear My Own Story

The Ba'al Shem Tov lay on his deathbed instructing his followers how they should carry on his legacy after he died. He told his faithful servant, Rabbi Jacob, "You will be a traveling storyteller, and tell stories far and wide of all the things you witnessed with me."

Rabbi Jacob's face fell. "You have decreed for me a difficult life," he said.

"Do not fear and do not complain," said the Ba'al Shem Tov. "You will not wander all your life. Eventually you will become wealthy. Look for this sign: when you tell someone a story, and he says 'You tell me a story about myself – I hear my own story', then you will know that your days of wandering are over."

The Ba'al Shem Tov passed away, and Rabbi Jacob fulfilled his master's instructions, traveling far and wide to tell wondrous tales of the great miracles which the Ba'al Shem Tov had performed.

One day, Rabbi Jacob heard of a wealthy Italian Jew who loved stories of the Ba'al Shem Tov so much that he would pay storytellers a gold coin for every one. Rabbi Jacob set out for Italy.

Rabbi Jacob arrived at the wealthy Jew's house and informed the guards that he had been the Ba'al Shem Tov's servant.

"Please be my guest for the Sabbath, and tell us all that you saw," said the master of the house. Rabbi Jacob accepted the offer, and word soon spread that the servant of the Ba'al Shem Tov himself would be telling wondrous tales at the communal Sabbath table.

At the Friday night meal, the host asked his honored guest to tell a story of the Ba'al Shem Tov. Rabbi Jacob opened his mouth to speak, but no words came out. He sat dumbstruck – he could not remember a single story! It was as if he had never known the Ba'al Shem Tov.

As the minutes ticked away, the townspeople murmured, "Perhaps he is a fraud."

The wealthy host looked disappointed, but reassured Rabbi Jacob, "You are no doubt tired from your journey. Have a good night's rest, and we will hear stories of the Ba'al Shem Tov tomorrow."

Rabbi Jacob went to his room and lay down, hoping that the darkness would restore his memory. But, try as he might, he could not even recall the face of his master, let alone any stories of his deeds. Rabbi Jacob wept all night.

The next day, at the Sabbath lunch table, the host again turned to Rabbi Jacob. "Perhaps you can now recall a story of your travels with the Ba'al Shem Tov?"

But Rabbi Jacob was still dumbstruck. "Nothing like this has ever happened to me before," he apologized.

The host's face fell but he said to Rabbi Jacob, "We will wait until the third Sabbath meal – perhaps you will recall a story by then."

But, at the third meal, Rabbi Jacob still could not recall a single story. The townspeople whispered to each other that he was a shameless liar.

It was clear to Rabbi Jacob that this forgetfulness was decreed from Heaven. "Perhaps," he thought to himself, "it is because the Ba'al Shem Tov decreed that I should be poor, and I came here hoping to become wealthy from my stories." Rabbi Jacob spent the rest of the Sabbath praying to God in despair.

The next morning, Rabbi Jacob bid farewell to his host. The man asked one last time, "Perhaps you can remember part of a story?"

Rabbi Jacob sadly shook his head. He rode off with a broken heart, trying to understand how he had merited this punishment.

Suddenly, Rabbi Jacob remembered an incident with the Ba'al Shem Tov. The driver took him back to his host, still standing with tears in his eyes. Rabbi Jacob ran to the man.

"I remember a story of the Ba'al Shem Tov!" he said in excitement.

"Tell me the story," said the Jew.

And here is the story that Rabbi Jacob told:

"One night the Ba'al Shem Tov took me with him on a journey. We drove all night long. At daybreak, we arrived at a city and stopped in front of a house with locked doors and closed shutters. I knocked on the door, and when no one answered, the Ba'al Shem Tov told me to knock harder.

Finally the door opened a crack, and an old woman whispered, 'Why are you here? Don't you know what day this is? The Bishop will be visiting our town today, and any Jew found in the street will be killed!'

We entered the house. Inside we found people hiding.

The Ba'al Shem Tov went to a window and threw open the shutter. We saw a large courtyard filled with people. At the far end of the courtyard was a platform with steps leading up to it.

Suddenly the Bishop's entourage rode into the court-yard. The Bishop climbed the steps to the platform.

His eyes glued to the Bishop, the Ba'al Shem Tov said to me 'Jacob, tell the Bishop I must talk with him.'

The inhabitants of the house protested, 'Are you mad? He'll be killed!' But the Ba'al Shem Tov assured me, 'Hurry, Jacob, do not be afraid.' I went to the platform and called up to the Bishop, 'The Ba'al Shem Tov is here, and he asks you to come speak with him.'

'I know he is here,' replied the Bishop. 'Tell him I will come after I deliver my speech.' I returned to the house and relayed the message.

The Ba'al Shem Tov was upset. 'Go back and tell the Bishop I need to talk with him *now!*'

And so I walked back through the crowd to the platform, where the Bishop had already started his speech. I tugged at the Bishop's robe to get his attention. 'The Ba'al Shem Tov says, *now!*'

The Bishop said to the crowd, 'Wait for me, I will return in a moment.' He followed me back to the house. The Ba'al Shem Tov and the Bishop went into a room, closed the door behind them, and spoke for hours. When the Ba'al Shem Tov emerged from the room, we got back in our wagon and drove away. What the Ba'al Shem Tov said, and what became of that Bishop, I do not know."

Rabbi Jacob looked up, his story done.

The wealthy Jew said to him, "Look at me – don't you recognize me? I was that Bishop. You tell me a story about myself – I hear my own story!"

"I was born a Jew," he continued, "but I was kidnapped and raised by a childless Gentile nobleman. I received a Christian education, and rose through the ranks to the position of Bishop. But the souls of my ancestors rescued me – they came to the Ba'al Shem Tov and begged him to bring me back to Judaism. And so, every night, the Ba'al Shem Tov would appear in my dreams, urging me to return to my people. Night after night this dream recurred, until I finally agreed to meet him. But I asked to postpone my repentance until after

I had given one final speech to the townspeople. The Ba'al Shem Tov refused, and sent you to stop me."

"In the room with him, I understood the error of my ways, and begged the Ba'al Shem Tov to teach me the path of repentance for all my sins. He taught me that path, and told me 'You will know your repentance has been accepted in Heaven when someone tells you your own story.'"

"I recognized you as soon as you arrived, and prayed that you would tell me my own story. When I saw that you could not remember I prayed for your memory to return. When you left, I understood that my repentance had not yet been accepted in Heaven, and I cried to God to accept my prayer."

"With God's help, you have remembered, and I have merited to hear my own story, which means I have been redeemed. You, Rabbi Jacob, need no longer earn your living telling stories. I will give you enough for you to live on all the rest of your days. And may the merit of the Ba'al Shem Tov protect us both."

The Right Story At The Right Time Can Redeem Both The Teller And The Listener

We humans are storytellers by nature. We tell stories to focus attention, build anticipation and leave a strong impression. But, as Rabbi Jacob learns, a story can do far more. It can be a source of livelihood, and it can have redemptive power, both for the audience and for the storyteller. A listener who feels as if he is hearing his own story may be transformed forever.

Effective managers must sometimes convince employees to change their behavior – to work harder, to work smarter, to cooperate with fellow employees. Managers often employ facts and rational arguments for this purpose. This approach sometimes backfires, eliciting a resistant counter-reaction

A less threatening approach is to employ stories. A story evokes emotions and can make the case for change in a non-confrontational way. It can ease people into unknown terrain by taking them there in their imaginations.

"Changing a diametrically opposed opinion demands that you move in baby steps," says Annette Simmons, author of *The Story Factor: Inspiration, Influence and Persuasion through Storytelling*.[14] "A story gives you the perfect format to gradually and indirectly move someone from one side of a conflict to the other side. Quoting research statistics, presenting philosophical arguments and delivering elegant rhetoric aims too high. You need to aim lower – underneath rational thought – and take smaller steps. If you can tell a story that makes sense to them, you can reframe the way they organize their thoughts, the meanings they draw, and thus the actions they take... People value their own conclusions more highly than yours... Once people make your story *their* story, you have tapped into the powerful force of faith."

In Today's World

Noel M. Tichy, a professor at the University of Michigan Business School and the co-author of *The Leadership Engine*[15], believes that telling stories is a key leadership skill. He says that leaders need to be adept at telling three kinds of stories:

- *Who am I?* These are the personal stories in which leaders describe the forces that shaped them. For example, Roberto Goizueta, chairman and CEO of the Coca Cola Corporation, often talked about his early days, when he was first exiled from Castro's Cuba and started over in a new country with $40 in cash and a hundred shares of Coca Cola stock. The lessons he learned about the importance of cash, the need to take risks, and the value of hard work guided him throughout his life, and sent a clear message to the entire organization about his values.

- *Who are we?* These are stories that articulate the shared beliefs of the team and their shared identity. For example, Chairman and CEO Phil Knight tells stories at Nike about the thrill of competing and winning as a runner. He thus sends a clear message to his employees that their goal is to help customers be winners in their athletic pursuits.
- *Where are we going?* These stories define the team's goals and how they can be achieved. For example, Martin Luther King's "I Have a Dream" speech galvanized an entire generation around the vision of black and white children holding hands in a second American Revolution.

Cognitive psychologist Gary Klein has discovered that stories play a key role in the decision-making process of experienced professionals in high-pressure fields such as fire-fighting and the military.

When faced with a crisis, expert decision-makers don't analyze and evaluate alternative options. Instead, they visualize a picture of the situation in their minds' eye, and tell themselves a story of how they would respond. If the simulation pans out, they act on it. If there is a problem with the mental scenario, they visualize a second story and, if it plays through successfully, implement that alternative.

When these experts mentor novices, they communicate their lessons by means of stories rather than analysis and logical breakdown.[16]

Judging by Klein's conclusions, a story is by far the most effective teaching tool a manager can employ.

41

Lesson 6: Every Question Has A Reason

What Should I Cook for Dinner?

Rabbi Abbele, the Chief Rabbi of Vilna, was sitting in his home one Thursday afternoon, surrounded by his students. The mood was boisterous and informal.

Their conversation was interrupted by a knock on the door. A young girl, dressed in the simple clothing of a servant, entered the room and approached the Rabbi hesitantly.

"Please excuse me for interrupting," she said. "I have a question."

"You are not interrupting at all," replied Rabbi Abbele in a kind voice. "Answering questions is one of my most important duties."

The students paused in their Talmudic discussion to listen to the girl's question.

"Rabbi, what should I cook for dinner?" she inquired with absolute seriousness.

All the students burst into uproarious laughter. They had been expecting to hear a religious or legal question, but instead the foolish girl was asking what she should cook for dinner! Was she mad or simply feeble-minded?

The students' derogatory howls were silenced by a stern glance from Rabbi Abbele, and they strained to hear their Rabbi's response.

"My dear," Rabbi Abbele said without a hint of sarcasm, "you should cook noodles."

"Thank you for your advice," the girl said. She curtsied and departed.

Rabbi Abbele's students could not believe their ears.

"Why did she ask such a trivial question, and why did you answer her?" they asked.

"Why are you so amazed?" asked Rabbi Abbele in return. "It is obvious from her attire that this girl is a servant in the home of a well-to-do family. And, from her question, it is obvious that she is a simple, trusting soul. I surmise that when the girl asked the mistress of the house, 'What should I cook for dinner?' the mistress sarcastically replied, 'Go ask the Rabbi!' This trusting girl did not realize that her mistress was rebuking her; she took the words literally and came here to ask me. Without insulting or embarrassing her, I gave her an answer which I hope will make both her and her mistress happy this evening."

There Is A Reason For Even The Strangest Question

Rabbi Abbele teaches his students a lesson in listening. It is not enough to hear or understand literally what someone is saying. Rabbi Abbele digs deeper to understand why the person asks what she does. What sort of personality, circumstances and assumptions would lead someone to make such a statement or ask such a question? Only through empathetic listening can Rabbi Abbele provide answers that will truly help his flock.

Rabbi Abbele teaches his students another, equally important lesson – to respect the dignity of every person, no matter how humble. Having inferred the servant girl's error, Rabbi Abbele does not confront or ridicule her. Instead, he provides an answer that preserves her self-respect.

A manager's listening skills, more than anything else, determine how successful he will be. The worst managers are poor listeners, whose subordinates are never really sure whether their reports are being understood or taken seriously.

A good manager is an active listener who takes care to fully understand the information his subordinates provide. And the best managers, like Rabbi Abbele, are empathetic listeners. Not satisfied with merely understanding what they hear from subordinates, they dig below the surface to understand *why* the situation is being reported in that way.

Most of your day as a manager is engaged in people telling you things. Besides the message they intend to communicate, their conversation conveys important information – their priorities, pet peeves, attitudes, self-image, fears, and desires. It's all there, if you ask the right questions and listen carefully. You may not have a degree in psychology, and you may sometimes hesitate to give too much weight to your analysis. But if you ignore warning signs from this type of indirect information, you may well regret it later.

In Today's World

An urban legend among salesmen tells of a man who went from one hardware store to the next, with the same strange request – "I want a round hole." Every clerk dismissed him as a pest and sent him on his way. Finally, the man wandered into the last hardware store in town, and declared, "I want a round hole." The clerk, who was a good listener and a quick thinker, responded, "We're all out of those today. But I've got a great deal on drill bits." The clerk made the sale, because he took the time to understand the customer and his problem.

Google.com is the Internet's most popular search engine and its home page is viewed by millions of people every day. Several years ago, an anonymous user began sending cryptic emails to Google's "comments" address. Each email contained only a two-digit number – no more, no less.

After several months, customer-support engineers decoded the meaning of these messages. Each email was an updated count of the number of words on Google's home page. Whenever the word count increased, it took longer for this Google zealot to download the home page. He expressed his irritation by informing Google of the newly elevated word count.

Now that they understand the message, the user interface team at Google finds this customer's email to be helpful feedback. It reminds them that their key performance index is download time, not graphic richness or number of advertising links[17].

Chapter Summary: Lessons in Motivating and Communicating from the Hasidic Masters

Here is a recap of the lessons from the stories in this chapter.

Motivating

- *To bring out the best in people, expect the best, but be willing to take the first penny.* Take what employees think they can give, then challenge them to meet ever-higher expectations.
- *Reward the team with pennies on the way to the big payoff.* Provide concrete, short-term tangible rewards for extraordinary effort, in addition to longer-term payoffs.
- *In times of stress, be there with your people.* Your team needs to know their effort is noticed and appreciated, and that you're not asking them to do something you are not willing to do yourself.
- *It may only take the smallest push to open a gate you assumed was locked.* Just taking the first step wins half the battle.
- *Your fate is not sealed. In fact, the answer is entirely in your hands.* Each and every team member needs to believe that success is achievable, and that the success of the project hangs on her individual effort.

Communicating

- A story can be the most effective way to convey a message and change behavior. *The right story at the right time can redeem both the teller and the listener.*
- Listen empathetically when your subordinates tell or ask you something; understand why they choose to discuss the situation as they do. *There is a reason for even the strangest question.*

CHAPTER 2

Setting Objectives

Dilbert, March 12, 2001

Rabbi Levi Yitzchak of Berditchev once saw a man running through the marketplace. Wishing to help, he asked, "Is someone chasing you?"

"No, Rebbe," responded the man breathlessly, "I am pursuing my livelihood."

Rabbi Levi looked puzzled. "How do you know that your livelihood lies in the direction you are running?" he asked. "Perhaps it is behind you, and you are in fact fleeing ever further from it?"

"A manager *sets objectives*. He determines what the objectives should be. He determines what the goals in each area of objectives should be. He decides what has to be done to reach those objectives. He makes the objectives effective by communicating them to the people whose performance is needed to attain them... Setting objectives... is a problem of balances... a balance between the immediate needs of the business and those of the future."[18]

- Peter F. Drucker

A Hasidic Rebbe is an agent for change. He is, by nature, never satisfied with things as they are, and constantly seeks to transform the mundane into the holy, to change people's lives by infusing them with more spirituality. The Rebbe charts strategic direction for his followers. How can they grow spiritually? How can they survive and thrive physically? How should they respond to external and internal challenges?

A manager, similarly, has the power and responsibility to establish objectives for the team and to optimize the chance of achieving them. The manager must look beyond the present reality to a vision of the future, determine which changes are needed in order to reach that vision, and must chart the course the team should travel. The manager must invest the resources of the team wisely in the efforts that will reap the greatest rewards.

Let's observe how the Hasidic Masters set objectives: charting strategy, determining when and what to change, and convincing followers that change is necessary.

SETTING STRATEGY

Lesson 7: Take The Long View

A Time To Cry, A Time To Laugh

Many years ago there lived a wealthy fur trader named Berel. Every year Berel traveled to the Great Fair in Leipzig where he bought enough furs to sell during the coming year.

One year, as the Great Fair approached, Berel placed all his money in a wooden box and set out for Leipzig with his servant, Meir. On the way they stopped in a meadow by the side of the road. Berel asked Meir to watch the moneybox and went off to find a quiet spot to pray the afternoon prayer. Meir was tired, so he covered the box with his hat and went to sleep beside it.

Some time later, Berel shouted, "Meir, wake up and let's continue on our way! It will soon be dark and this forest is full of robbers!" Meir jumped up, ran to the wagon and drove off, leaving behind his hat and the moneybox.

"Thank God we had a safe journey," said Berel to Meir when they arrived in Leipzig two days later. "Where is the money you have been guarding?"

Meir's heart sank. "I left it under my hat in the meadow!" he blurted, and burst into tears. Berel stared at his servant in disbelief.

Words cannot describe Berel's anguish. He had lost his entire fortune and had gone from affluence to poverty overnight. Meir was wracked by guilt over the ruin he had brought on his master.

"Perhaps," Meir suggested hopefully, "the money is still there by the side of the road under my hat."

"Do you have any idea how many travelers pass by that meadow on the way to the Great Fair?" asked Berel. "Certainly someone has spotted your hat and taken the chest by now. There is no chance that it is still there. My only hope is to buy furs at the fair on credit."

Berel tried all week to buy on credit at the Great Fair, but none of the fur traders were willing to sell. Broken-hearted, Berel and Meir left Leipzig to return home.

Along the way, they passed by the meadow. Gazing out into the pasture, Meir saw a shadow on the grass. He ran from the wagon, with Berel close behind. It was his hat, and the wooden box was still there! Meir opened it and discovered the money, intact.

The servant was ecstatic. So many people had passed by, and no one had disturbed the hat. What a miracle! His master was saved. But when Meir looked around, he saw Berel sitting on the ground, crying as if in mourning.

"What is the matter, master?" asked Meir. "Why are you crying? See what fortune God has brought you!"

"Leave me! I do not want you to be my servant any longer!" sobbed Berel. "Take half the money and go!"

Meir thought his poor master had gone mad, but Berel insisted until Meir took half the money, and they parted ways.

Berel returned home but his luck had changed and all his business deals failed until he went bankrupt. He joined a group of itinerant beggars, wandering from town to town.

One day the beggars came to a certain town where Berel knocked on the door of a grand home. He was surprised when the master of the house gave him a gold coin.

"I will give you another gold coin," said the wealthy man, "if you will be my guest for the Sabbath." Berel agreed to this unusual request and left.

Berel showed the beggars his gold coin, and told of his Sabbath invitation and the promise of yet another gold coin. The beggars were jealous of Berel's good fortune, and devised a plan to teach him a lesson.

On Friday the beggars went to the public bathhouse to prepare for the Sabbath. While Berel was bathing, the other beggars stole his clothes.

"Let's see the honored Sabbath guest now," snickered the ringleader.

When Berel came out of the bath he looked for his clothes, but they were nowhere to be found. By now the bathhouse attendant was impatient to lock up. Berel had no clothes, but the attendant insisted that he leave. Naked and desperate, Berel ran to a nearby garden and covered himself with leaves.

When Sabbath came the wealthy man went to the synagogue and looked in vain for his guest. He returned home and waited for an hour, then set out to search for the beggar in town. As he passed the ritual bath he heard noise from a garden across the street and followed the sound into the foliage. He was shocked to discover his beggar guest, covered in leaves, singing and dancing joyously!

"Look at my face," he said to Berel the beggar. "Don't you recognize me? I am Meir, your faithful servant! Your ordeal has driven you mad!"

"I am not mad," said Berel. "I thank God that at least He has left me my sanity. And now He has sent me you!"

"God has been with me in my business," said Meir, "and I want to repay your money. But first, please explain your behavior. Why, when we found the box of money in the meadow, did you cry as if you were mourning the destruction of the Holy Temple? And why are you now rejoicing as if you were celebrating the giving of the Torah?"

"I will explain," said Berel. "When, against all odds, we found the money in the meadow, I knew that I had reached the peak of my good fortune and that it could only decline from there, so I mourned. I gave you half my money so that at least some of my wealth would be saved. This evening, finding myself penniless and naked, I recognized that I had reached bottom. Things could only improve from here. I rejoiced because I know that God can bring salvation in the twinkling of an eye. And so He has!"

Meir repaid Berel the money he had given him. From then on, God restored Berel's good fortune.

Learn To Cry During Triumphs And Laugh During Disasters

Berel has a unique perspective that takes him beyond the emotions of the moment. Because he understands the implications of his inordinate good luck, he can plan ahead. By recognizing the nadir of his fortune, he also survives his trauma. His dislocation in time may look like madness, but it is, in fact, the product of his wisdom and the source of his strength.

A manager often experiences a dislocation in time, living ahead of the news of the moment. While everyone else is celebrating the signing of a new contract, the Vice President of Engineering may be worrying about how his organization will deliver the product on time. When a business deal falls through and the atmosphere is gloom and doom, the CEO may feel optimistic because she's already on the trail of a bigger and better business opportunity.

This is one of a manager's most vital roles: providing perspective beyond the moment and planning for eventualities that are not yet evident to others. Other employees whose job is to live in the present and solve the here-and-now problems typically don't have this view. A good manager thinks ahead and lives sometime in the future.

In Today's World

"Getting off the dance floor and going to the balcony" is what Ronald Heifitz and Martin Linsky call this ability to maintain perspective in the midst of action. Step back from the fray and ask, "What's really going on here?"

"Sustaining good leadership requires first and foremost the capacity to see what is happening to you and your initiative as it is happening, and to understand how today's turns in the road will affect tomorrow's plans."[19]

It's natural to get swept up in the action, especially when it becomes intense or personal. You need to climb up to the balcony to pick up patterns, to notice how your behavior is influencing the discussion, to look at relationships and see how people are supporting or thwarting each other. As Yogi Berra said, "You observe a lot by watching."

It can be tempting to stay up in the balcony. But after you have spotted the patterns, you have to return to the dance floor and act based on your perspective. The process must be iterative, alternating between analysis and action.

For centuries, religious traditions have taught disciplines that encourage followers to reflect during action. Jesuits call it *contemplation in action*; the Hindus refer to it as *Karma Yoga*, the yoga of action.

Simultaneous observation and participation is difficult, say Heifitz and Linsky, but it can be learned. For example, when you make a point during a meeting, resist the instinct to perch on the edge of your seat, poised to defend your position. Instead, simply push your chair back a few inches from the table after you speak. This encourages other participants to interpret and react to your point. Watch and listen carefully to gather new information from which to form a more reflective perspective. When you are ready, re-enter the fray and endorse a particular strategy or decision, one that has benefited from your and your colleagues' new point of view.

Faith in a better future gives great managers the strength to tough it out during trying times, according to management researcher Jim Collins.[20]

Admiral James Stockdale miraculously survived seven years of brutal torture in a Vietcong prisoner-of-war camp. His unbreakable character set an example for the other prisoners, and he was personally responsible for the survival of many men who would have perished without his influence. How did Stockdale survive for seven years?

He did not view himself as an optimist. "The optimists were the ones who said 'We're going to be out by Christmas', and Christmas would come and Christmas would go. Then they'd say, 'We're going to be home by Easter', and Easter would come and Easter would go... and then it would be Christmas again, and they died of a broken heart."

To survive, Stockdale embraced two seemingly contradictory beliefs known as the Stockdale Paradox: confront the most brutal facts of the current situation, but retain faith that you will triumph in the end, regardless of the difficulties.

British Prime Minister Winston Churchill succeeded in conveying two such contradictory messages during the darkest days of World War II. In the short term, he acknowledged that there would be "blood, toil, tears and sweat." But he communicated an optimistic certainty that England would prevail, "however long and hard the road may be."

Collins uses the Stockdale Paradox to describe a key trait found in top business leaders. They deal realistically with the brutal threats confronting the company, while at the same time transmitting their overarching conviction that ultimately the company will realize its vision. They are able to sustain the tension between facts and faith.[21]

Lesson 8: There's More Than One Winning Strategy

The Rabbi's Advice

Once there was a Jewish innkeeper who did not believe in the power of Hasidic Rabbis, while his wife believed they could work miracles.

Every year the innkeeper owed a hefty rent fee to the local Prince for the privilege of running the inn. The innkeeper's rent payment was higher than the amount he earned from selling liquor to local peasants and lodging to passing travelers, and he had not paid the Prince the rent fee for the past three years. The exasperated Prince threatened the Jew with a deadline – if the innkeeper could not pay by that date, the Prince would throw him and his family into jail.

"I hear that Rabbi Israel of Rozhin performs miracles," said the innkeeper's wife. "Go to him for help."

The innkeeper laughed bitterly. "I don't need miracles, I need money! Does the Rabbi of Rozhin hand out money to strangers?"

The deadline approached and the innkeeper despaired. His wife pleaded with him to go.

"If you believe so much in this Rabbi, go see him yourself!" said the innkeeper.

So the wife traveled to Rozhin to make her request to the Rabbi. When she arrived at his court she was ushered into a waiting room.

"What brings you here? And how will so many people see the Rabbi?" she asked the woman next to her.

"There are too many people for the Rabbi to meet individually," the woman replied, "so each person writes down his request. The Rabbi reads them and writes responses for his secretary to distribute. As for me, my husband is deathly ill, and as the doctors offer no hope, I am here to seek the Rabbi's advice."

The innkeeper's wife and the woman wrote their requests and waited. It happened on this occasion that the secretary accidentally mixed up the responses. The woman with the sick husband received the response, "I will pray that God may help you," while the innkeeper's wife received the response, "Apply leeches and all will be well."

The innkeeper's wife knew that leeches were reputed to suck out "bad blood" and stimulate the body to produce "good blood," but this did not seem to be relevant financial advice. However, her innocent faith in the Rabbis overcame any doubts she might have otherwise had.

The wife returned home and told her husband, "The Rabbi of Rozhin says to apply leeches."

The innkeeper howled with bitter laughter. "I told you the Rabbis are useless fools. I don't need leeches! I need money!"

The fateful day dawned. The innkeeper sat listlessly awaiting his destiny.

His wife pleaded with him, "We are surely lost. What more can you lose by following the Rabbi's advice?" The innkeeper consented to his wife's application of leeches. After a few hours, she removed them and left her husband bleeding in his bed.

The Prince's messengers arrived to collect the rent. They asked the innkeeper's wife "Where is the Prince's money?"

She sadly shook her head and murmured, "It's not here."

"Where is your husband?" asked the messengers. She put a finger to her lips and silently led them to the innkeeper, lying weak and bloody in his bed. The messengers were shocked by his appearance and rushed back to inform the Prince that the Jew was bloody and beaten and at death's doorstep.

The Prince wanted to see for himself. "Bring him to me!" he commanded. The messengers returned to the inn and brought back the innkeeper, pale and weak, soaked in his own blood.

The Prince was shocked at the sight of the Jew. "What happened to you?" he asked. The innkeeper was too weak to respond.

One of the messengers spoke up. "His wife said their money is gone. Look at this man's state – he obviously put up a good fight with his attackers!"

The Prince took pity on the poor Jew. "I see that you fought valiantly to prevent robbers from taking the money you owe me. I hereby excuse your rent debt for the past three years. And, because you were beaten while protecting my property, I release you from paying rent for the next three years. Use the time to recover your health and revive your business."

And so the innkeeper and his wife traveled to the Rabbi of Rozhin to express their gratitude for the blessing that had saved them. When they told him their story, the Rabbi realized what had happened.

"When I read your request, I saw that there was no way I could help you, so I gave you a general blessing that God should help. I certainly would never have ordered you to apply leeches – the secretary mixed up the responses. But your wife's complete faith in the Rabbis – that is truly what has brought you salvation from God."

If Executed With Total Commitment, Even Applying Leeches Can Be A Winning Strategy

At a strategic crossroad, it's the job of the manager to choose a plan and motivate the team to execute it. There's always a lingering doubt, both for the manager and the team – did we make the right choice? In some cases, this doubt can be demoralizing or paralyzing. As the story illustrates, identifying the one perfect strategy can be overrated, since there is probably more than one winning strategy. Sometimes, even if you choose a less than ideal path, total commitment and flawless execution can bring about the desired outcome.

In Today's World

Many people forget that IBM launched the first commercially successful personal computer. Why, then, did IBM never become a market leader in the multi-billion-dollar PC industry? The answer: flawed execution. IBM's process for releasing new products was so slow and laborious that Lou Gerstner, IBM's CEO, once commented, "IBM products aren't launched, but they occasionally manage to escape."[22] Neither did the company believe that a significant percentage of the world's computing workload would ever migrate from IBM's behemoth mainframes to personal computers. Despite having great technology and a great product, IBM failed to execute, leaving a colossal market to upstarts like Dell, Compaq and Microsoft.

Nowadays we take for granted the standard *WIMP* (windows, icons, mouse, pull-down menus) interface with which we interact with our computers – a mouse cursor points at folders and icons on a virtual desktop. Who invented this desktop metaphor? It wasn't Microsoft, the company that's derived the most profit from it – they borrowed the idea from Steve Jobs' Apple Macintosh.

But the story doesn't end there. Apple itself borrowed the concept from another company that we do not usually associate with personal computers – Xerox. Their Palo Alto Research Center, Xerox PARC, invented this interface, as well as many of the basic technologies we associate with the personal computer – the first bitmap monitor capable of displaying graphics, the laser printer, the Ethernet networking interface used to connect computers, and more. Why, then, was Xerox unable to capitalize on this opportunity?

The answer: flawed execution. Xerox management invested in research, but they were too focused on the photocopier market to recognize that they had stumbled upon an even greater opportunity. As a result, Xerox missed their chance to become a dominant player in the PC market.[23]

JetBlue discount airline was launched while established carriers were bleeding red ink. JetBlue's David Neeleman has succeeded where others have failed, largely due to flawless execution. Consider:

- JetBlue is rated number one in on-time departures, with 99% of its flights leaving on time.
- From August 6 to September 15, 2002, JetBlue flew 20,000 flights without a single cancellation.
- Dave Barger, JetBlue's president, receives daily reports on how long it takes each piece of luggage to reach the

baggage carousel. He strives to ensure that no customer waits more than twenty minutes for his bag.

The result? Even during a difficult period in the economy, JetBlue achieved $600 million in sales in its second full year of operation.[24]

PLANNING CHANGE

Lesson 9: There Is Not Always A Better Alternative

The Least Flawed Alternative

Little Shlomo was born deaf and mute. The finest doctors were unable to suggest a cure. In desperation, Shlomo's parents brought the boy before Rabbi Moshe Zvi of Sevarin.

"Please, Rebbe," they implored, "we are not Hasidim, but we have heard that you perform wonders and that God Himself heeds your prayers. Our son cannot hear or speak. Please bless him that he may be cured."

Rabbi Moshe Zvi took little Shlomo's hand, stared into his eyes, and said to him, "If you could talk, what would you say when you grew up?"

Shlomo's father shook his head. "What sort of miracle worker is this," he thought to himself, "who ignores the reality of the boy's condition, and addresses our son as if he can hear and speak?"

The father's thoughts were interrupted by the unfamiliar sound of Shlomo's voice.

"When I grow up," the boy said in a loud, clear voice, "I would be an informer, selling information about my fellow Jews to the authorities."

Rabbi Moshe Zvi released the boy's hand and stood up. "I could cure your son," he said to Shlomo's parents, "but I do not wish to do so. It is better for him to remain silent."

Shlomo resumed his silence, and never spoke another word for the rest of his days.

The Current Situation, With All Its Flaws, May Be The Best Available Alternative

Shlomo's parents, understandably, would do anything in their power to enable their son to hear and speak. Rabbi Moshe Zvi shows them that, though the status quo may seem tragic, it is, in fact, the preferable alternative for Shlomo, his parents and his fellow man.

At a strategic juncture where you must determine whether to make a change or maintain the status quo, it is your job as a manager to extrapolate the consequences of the available alternatives. You may wish that you possessed a miracle-worker's supernatural ability to predict the consequences of potential change. Your only certainty may be that the current situation is painful. But Rabbi Moshe Zvi teaches that the present situation, no matter how difficult, may be better than the alternatives. A wrong decision could, in fact, make things so much worse that everyone would look back fondly at today's problems as "the good old days."

Execute the change only if you are convinced that it has a reasonable chance to produce a better world, with clear tangible improvements over the current situation.

In Today's World

The most profound and far-reaching change at the corporate level is a merger. The past decade has brought a number of mega-unions, with two companies reorganizing into a single corporate entity, hoping to benefit from potential synergies (the elusive "1+1=3" effect). Looking back, we can see that many of these mega-mergers have created more problems than they solved.

- In May 1998, Germany's Daimler-Benz and the Chrysler Corporation merged to form the fifth largest automaker in the world. On paper, the merger looked like a perfect marriage, combining top-notch German engineering and American creativity into a global company large enough to benefit from economies of scale. In reality, the troubled union tarnished Mercedes' reputation, produced huge losses at Chrysler ($2 billion in 2001), and diminished shareholder value.[25]
- In January 2000, America Online and Time-Warner merged in a marriage of old and new media titans. Executives hoped that the combination of Time-Warner's media properties (e.g., Time Magazine, Warner Studios) and cable systems, together with AOL's Internet savvy and reach, would not only merge two industries, but would give birth to a new industry alogether.[26] Looking back in the wake of the burst Internet bubble, regulatory restrictions, and fierce clashes of corporate culture, it appears that "1+1" has added up to significantly less than two, let alone three.

These mergers are, at best, works in progress that may still yield future rewards. But, perhaps there are managers in these companies who have come to realize that the pre-merger environment, with all its flaws and challenges, may in fact have been a world with a more harmonious and workable balance.

This does not mean to imply that all mergers are ill-advised or doomed to failure. In 2003 Hewlett-Packard acquired Compaq Computers in order to "offer the industry's most complete set of IT products and services for both businesses and consumers."[27] The merger appears to be achieving its goal by creating a one-stop market leader in the PC market and the computer service business.

Making this merger work, however, has required Herculean effort and an iron will from Carly Fiorina, HP's talented CEO, first to convince shareholders, then to integrate the companies' product lines and strategies, and ultimately to convince consumers that the new "HP way" makes sense. Perhaps this exception proves the rule by illustrating just how hard it is to make change succeed on this scale.

Lesson 10: Change What Matters

For Hundreds of Years

Czar Nikolai I ruled nineteenth century Russia with an iron fist and demanded unflinching loyalty from all his subjects. He was especially harsh with the Jews of Russia, for he suspected that their true allegiance was to their rabbinic leaders rather than the Czar.

Nikolai ordered the establishment of a puppet "Chief Rabbinic Assembly," consisting of two leading Rabbinic authorities: Rabbi Isaac of Volozhin and Rabbi Menachem Mendel of Lubavitch. Nikolai believed that through this assembly he could promulgate his decrees among the Jews. But he underestimated the determination and cleverness of Rabbi Isaac and Rabbi Menachem Mendel.

Once, at a meeting of the Grand Rabbinic Assembly in Saint Petersburg, the Russian Minister of Education told Rabbi Isaac, "I am told that in your synagogues, on the Jewish New Year, you Jews recite a prayer that 'all the wickedness of this world should evaporate like smoke'. My informers tell me that when Jews utter this prayer they have in mind the government of our Czar Nikolai. This is treason! In the name of the Czar, I demand that the Great Rabbinic Assembly strike this prayer from Jewish prayer books and from the New Year service."

Rabbi Menachem calmly responded, "In my opinion, there is no need to change the prayer. The government can leave the prayer book and the service as they are."

The Minister was outraged. "You Jews openly call for the Czar's downfall, and expect us to leave the prayer as it is?"

Rabbi Menachem responded, "Your Honor, you misunderstand. The Jews are not calling for a revolution, they are merely expressing their hope for a tranquil world at the end of days. Why should it matter to you whether we leave this prayer in our prayer books? Look at it this way: for hundreds of years, Jews have been praying that prayer with complete devotion. Has it helped?"

Change Substance, Not Symbols

The Russian Minister mistakenly assumes that the prayers are a here-and-now call for a Jewish revolt, and therefore need to be changed. Rabbi Menachem points out that, while the prayers do matter to the Jews, expressing a plea to God for freedom, they transcend time and therefore need not (and do not) disturb the Russian government. They are hardly a concrete threat, nor a call to arms.

Rabbi Menachem's argument is cynical but powerful: if you want to change the here and now, make sure you are changing things that matter here and now, and not symbols or long-term aspirations.

A Divine Arrangement

Once in Safed there lived a sincere but unlearned Marrano, a "hidden Jew" from Portugal who had been forcibly converted to Christianity. He had come to Safed to return to his Jewish roots, and though he was ignorant of Jewish learning, he had great respect for the mystics who came to Safed to study with the Holy Rabbi Isaac Luria, the undisputed master of Jewish spirituality.

The Marrano's rabbi, Rabbi Eliav, gave a sermon one Sabbath about the Shewbread, the two loaves of consecrated bread which the priests would offer in the Holy Temple every Sabbath.

"All this happened when our Holy Temple stood," said Rabbi Eliav. "Now, due to our sins, the Temple has been destroyed and the Lord has no more Shewbread."

The Marrano was deeply saddened by the thought of the Lord being left without bread. After the Sabbath service, he went home and told his wife, "Rabbi Eliav says that the Lord has not been served bread since the Holy Temple was destroyed. There is no bread as delicious as the bread you bake for the Sabbath. Next week, please bake two extra loaves and I will present them to God. I know we are poor and unworthy, but perhaps God will accept our gift."

His wife, as unlearned and trusting as he, agreed. Later that week, she bought the finest flour, mixed and kneaded the dough, and braided two beautiful loaves.

The next Friday, the Marrano went to the synagogue after the morning service with two loaves under his coat. He opened the doors of the Holy Ark and carefully placed the two loaves next to the Torah scrolls. "God, please accept these two loaves," he prayed, "and may they find favor before You." He closed the Ark and left the synagogue.

A short time later, the caretaker entered the synagogue to clean floors, arrange books, and set up candles in preparation for the Sabbath. The congregation was poor and paid the simple, pious caretaker a paltry salary. This week he did not even have enough to buy a Sabbath meal for his family.

The caretaker went to the Ark to arrange the Torah scrolls. As he kissed the curtain that covered the Ark, he prayed to God, "Please help me provide my family with the Sabbath meal." He opened the Ark and discovered two fragrant loaves! He assumed that God had answered his prayer, and brought the loaves home to his family who rejoiced at God's gift of a worthy Sabbath meal.

As the sun began to set, the Marrano went to the synagogue early to see what had become of the two loaves he had left for God. He opened the Ark. It was empty!

The Marrano was overjoyed – his wife's loaves had found favor in God's eyes! He said the Sabbath evening prayers with love and reverence. When he returned to his home, he said to his wife, "Praise the Lord, who does not despise the gift of the poor. He took your bread from the Ark! Now that we see that your bread is pleasing to the Lord, let us make this gift to Him every week."

And so, the following week and for many years following, the scenario repeated itself. Each man, in his sincerity and simplicity, believed that God Himself was answering his prayers.

One Friday morning, Rabbi Eliav happened to stay in the synagogue to prepare his sermon after the morning prayers. He was sitting quietly, reviewing his speech in the far corner of the synagogue, when he heard the door of the synagogue open. The Marrano walked in carrying two loaves of bread. The Rabbi watched quietly as the Marrano opened the Ark and placed the loaves inside.

"Oh, God," he heard the Marrano say, "may these loaves be pleasing to You, and may You take them and find them savory, as You have taken my humble gift in the past."

"Fool!" bellowed Rabbi Eliav, "Do you think that the God of Israel is flesh and blood, that He eats bread? This is a great sin!"

The Marrano was startled and stammered, "But, Rabbi, you once said that God misses the Shewbread He used to have in the Temple. I didn't want God to be without bread, so each week I bring Him two loaves, and God takes my gift."

"You ignorant fool," said the rabbi with scorn. "Come sit with me in the back of the synagogue, and we shall see who takes your loaves."

Rabbi Eliav and the Marrano sat in the far corner of the synagogue until the door opened and the caretaker entered. They watched silently as the caretaker said a prayer to God, opened the Ark and took the loaves.

The Rabbi strode to the front of the synagogue. "Besides thanking God, you should thank this man for your weekly Sabbath bread," he berated the caretaker. "It's not God who puts your bread in the Ark every week – it's this man here! Why, this is blasphemy! Do you think God bakes bread or has arms to carry loaves?"

The Marrano and the caretaker both wept. The Marrano asked Rabbi Eliav's forgiveness for having misunderstood his sermon. The caretaker pleaded with Rabbi Eliav to suggest a way to repent for his unintentional sin. The two men left, brokenhearted.

The Rabbi returned to the sermon he was preparing, satisfied that he had properly rebuked two ridiculous simpletons.

A short time later, a student of the Holy Rabbi Isaac Luria, Chief Rabbi of Safed, came to the synagogue with a message for Rabbi Eliav.

"Prepare yourself and your household. Tomorrow, at the time when you intend to deliver your sermon, you will die. The decree has gone out from Heaven."

Rabbi Eliav rushed to Rabbi Isaac's study hall and asked, "What is my sin that I have merited such a harsh decree?"

Rabbi Isaac answered, "I heard from the angels that this decree was issued because you destroyed God's arrangement with the Marrano and the caretaker. In doing so, you thwarted God's pleasure. From the day the Holy Temple was destroyed, God had no greater pleasure than to see the Marrano give Him the bread and the caretaker take the bread from Him with innocent sincerity. Each man truly believed that God Himself was his partner. And so it was – each was God's messenger to the other. Because you destroyed their simple sincerity, you have been decreed to die. The decree cannot be overturned, just as the innocence of the Marrano and the caretaker cannot be returned."

Rabbi Eliav accepted the decree and went home to prepare himself and his family. Rabbi Eliav died the next day at the time when he was to have delivered his Sabbath sermon.

Don't Rush To Judge The Harmony Of The Grand Plan

In the previous story Rabbi Menachem instructed us to focus change on those things that really make a difference. Rabbi Eliav has a different problem: he tries to fix something that isn't broken. Undone by hubris, with no respect for human feelings or faith, he swoops in to correct what he considers primitive behavior, unaware that he is, in fact, destroying an exquisite balance.

As a manager, before you set out to change or improve something, make sure you really understand how it works today, and make sure it really is something that matters. Perhaps what appears, on the surface, to be something that must be changed is actually part of a delicately interconnected mechanism that will not tolerate tinkering, or is a red herring that has nothing to do with the real here-and-now problem.

In Today's World

The Coca Cola Corporation introduced "New Coke" in 1985 with an announcement that it was changing its long-time formula. For several years, Coke had been on the verge of losing the Cola War to Pepsi, with diminishing market share and flat sales. Pepsi-Cola had conducted the "Pepsi Challenge" taste test across America in 1984-1985 and was heavily advertising its findings: more people preferred the sweet, smooth taste of Pepsi over the sharp, biting taste of Coke.

Robert Goizueta, Coca Cola's chairman, pressed the panic button. Coca Cola's internal test had confirmed Pepsi's findings. So Goizueta commissioned his team to formulate a "Pepsi-killer," with a smoother, sweeter taste than the original Coke. Results from a battery of tests showed that people liked the new formula better than both the old Coke and Pepsi, by a significant factor.

On April 23, 1985, Goizueta announced the launch of New Coke and declared that production of the original formula would end that same week. Customer outrage was immediate and fierce. In Seattle, Gay Mullins founded The Old Coke Drinkers of America and set up a hotline for angry consumers. Disgruntled customers staged protests and threatened class action suits. A Beverly Hills wine merchant bought 500 cases of "vintage" Coke and sold them at a premium.[28]

Meanwhile, the Coca Cola Company was receiving 1,500 phone calls a day along with van loads of mail from irate customers. One Coke loyalist wrote that changing Coke was "akin to diddling with the U.S. Constitution." Another wrote, "Changing Coke is like God making the grass purple."

Three months later, Coca Cola bowed to public pressure, and announced the return of the old formula, under the name "Coca Cola Classic." Donald Keough, the company's President, said "The simple fact is that all the time and money and skill poured into consumer research on the new Coca Cola could not measure or reveal the deep and abiding emotional attachment to original Coca Cola felt by so many people. The passion for original Coca Cola was something that caught us by surprise... It is a wonderful American mystery... and you cannot measure it, any more than you can measure love, pride or patriotism."[29]

Why did the Coca Cola Company attempt such a risky product change? It appears that they did not understand the real source of their customers' attachment to Coke. It has nothing to do with taste, and everything to do with the power of brands to inspire customer loyalty. Coca Cola is an American icon, and their ad campaigns have, for almost a century, convinced consumers that Coke captures the spirit of America and is a central part of the American experience. Instead of performing market research on taste comparisons, the Coca Cola Corporation should have been asking test subjects how they would feel if the New Coke were to replace the old one.

In the long run, Coca Cola's "punishment" for changing a system they did not really understand was less drastic than Rabbi Eliav's. After an initial dip in sales following the New Coke fiasco, Classic Coke re-captured the cola crown from Pepsi in early 1986. Ironically, the threat of replacing the original formula with a new one turned out to be exactly what Coca Cola needed to revitalize itself. "It took the loss of the beverage people had grown up with and fallen in love over to remind them how much it meant to them. No longer taken for granted, Coca Cola had been reaffirmed in their affection." [30]

CHANGING PEOPLE

Lesson 11: Change Must Come From Within

How to Change a Mind

Young Laybel Eiger was a fortunate young man of distinguished lineage who had grown up in the lap of luxury. To top it off, God had blessed Laybel with a brilliant mind. At the age of seven, the boy was already studying Talmud and the fine points of Jewish law with Lublin's leading teachers, and by the time he turned fourteen, Laybel was known throughout Poland as one of the generation's most promising young scholars.

He received many offers from wealthy Jews who wished for such a worthy son-in-law. His father chose for him the daughter of Rabbi Azriel Gradstein.

Rabbi Gradstein was of the mainstream school of Judaism and viewed Hasidism as a dangerous cult that ruined the innocent by encouraging them to abandon worldly concerns, such as family and livelihood, and devote themselves entirely to spiritual pursuits. To protect the young couple against the lure of Hasidism, he inserted a special clause into the marriage contract explicitly forbidding Laybel from any contact with Hasidim.

After the wedding, Laybel settled into a life devoted to Talmudic study. Word of the brilliant young scholar from Lublin reached Rabbi Menachem Mendel, the Hasidic Rabbi of Kotsk.

"A soul as great as Laybel's belongs in Kotsk," declared Rabbi Menachem. He set about planning ways to attract the young scholar to Hasidism.

The mission was difficult. Laybel spent all his days in the study hall, plumbing the depths of the Talmud, and he meticulously honored his commitment to abjure contact with Hasidim.

Rabbi Menachem sent his most articulate disciples to the study hall and instructed them to draw Laybel into conversation. The Hasidim sat at the table next to Laybel and embarked on an intricate discussion of the fine points of a complex Talmudic passage.

Laybel overheard their arguments with interest. He was about to interject a clarification that would have resolved their deliberation, but, remembering his marriage pledge, he swallowed his words and walked away.

Rabbi Menachem was not easily deterred. He patiently awaited the proper moment. It came on Yom Kippur, the holiest day of the year, when Jews fast and pray for forgiveness.

At midnight, long after the rest of the congregation had gone home to sleep, Laybel sat alone in the study hall, learning the laws of repentance by the light of a flickering candle. Absorbed in his study, Laybel did not notice when a Jew dressed in soiled work clothes entered and sat at the next table.

Laybel glanced up and saw that he was no longer alone. He recognized Eliezer of Bialystok, one of Rabbi Menachem's most famous students. But why was he here at this hour? And why was he dressed in such an unbefitting manner? Remembering his promise to his father-in-law, Laybel turned back to his book and tried to absorb himself in study.

Eliezer also took a book from the table, and absent-mindedly turned the pages for a few moments. Then, to Laybel's amazement, Eliezer lay down on the bench and fell fast asleep.

Eliezer's echoing snores enraged Laybel. Was this the way a Jew should act in the study hall? And on Yom Kippur of all days! As Laybel fumed, the door burst open with a bang and in walked several young men whom Laybel recognized as followers of Rabbi Menachem.

Talking loudly and joking among themselves, the group of boors sat down at Eliezer's table. Laybel ignored them and they ignored him as well. They began to sing a Kotsk melody, which awakened Eliezer.

Sitting up on the bench, Eliezer rubbed his eyes, turned to one of his fellow Hasidim and said, "This calls for a toast! Do you have any whiskey?" The Hasid pulled a bottle of whiskey from one pocket and glasses from another.

Laybel's consternation turned to shock. Had these Hasidim forgotten that today was Yom Kippur, when food and drink was forbidden? He was about to rebuke them when he again remembered his promise to his father-in-law.

As Laybel sat in stunned silence, Eliezer brought the glass full of whiskey towards his lips, and began to recite the prescribed blessing before drinking, "Blessed art Thou.... "

Laybel could no longer contain himself. To prevent a Jew from committing such a heinous sin was surely more important than any promise. Jumping from his seat, he shouted, "Stop! Have you gone mad?"

Eliezer lowered the glass from his mouth. Turning to Laybel, he said innocently, "What is all the fuss about?"

"Today is Yom Kippur!" blurted Laybel.

"And what if it is?" asked Eliezer calmly. "What's the harm in drinking a little whiskey on Yom Kippur?

Who says it's forbidden?"

"What sort of question is that?" snorted Laybel. "The Torah commands us to fast and deny ourselves any pleasure on this day!"

"Well," said Eliezer reflectively, "what if the Torah does forbid it? So what?"

"So what!" fumed Laybel. "The Torah was given by God Himself, and contains His holy commandments!"

"Even so," responded Eliezer, "who is God that I should fear Him or obey Him?"

Laybel was nonplussed. "But... because... how... ," he stammered. He'd never even heard such a question before, a direct challenge to the beliefs on which he had been raised. He had immersed himself in the legalistic arguments of the Talmud from an early age, and had never thought about such basic philosophical questions.

Now, in the study hall at midnight on Yom Kippur, his world had been turned upside down in an instant, and he had no answer to a question he'd never considered.

Eliezer put his arm around Laybel's shoulder and looked into his eyes. "Young man," he said, "if you desire to know who God is and why you should obey His commandments – travel with us to Kotsk! Today is Yom Kippur, when God frees man from any rash vows made during the year. Your promise to refrain from contact with Hasidim is null and void, like the dust of the earth."

Rabbi Menachem's plan succeeded. Laybel traveled to Kotsk and became a devoted follower of Rabbi Menachem.

You Can't Change A Person – You Can Only Make Him Want To Change

R abbi Menachem wishes to cause a transformation in outlook that will convert Laybel to Hasidism. To effect this change, he seeks to catalyze in Laybel an epiphany, a flash of recognition. In order to truly change, Laybel must himself realize that the present direction is flawed, and choose, of his own accord, to abandon it in favor of a better way. Perhaps Rabbi Menachem could have employed other techniques – intellectual persuasion, confrontation, a show of authority. But Rabbi Menachem knows that none of these will have the same deep and long-lasting effect as a spontaneous and autonomous discovery.

Paradoxically, bringing about that "spontaneous" moment in a disciple requires Rabbi Menachem to lay intricate groundwork. Months of gathering information, devising a plan, instructing a team in how to execute the plan – all in order to bring Laybel to that single moment of recognition.

This is good advice for any manager seeking to convince an employee to change his established ways of thinking and behaving. Plan carefully and look for the opportunity to create a spontaneous moment of independent discovery, the realization by the employee or team that change is required.

In Today's World

You cannot motivate problem employees – only they themselves can do that. This is the conclusion reached by Nigel Nicholson after thirty years of studying business organizations, as described in his article "How to Motivate Your Problem People."[31] The manager's job, in Nicholson's view, is to create the circumstances in which an employee's inherent motivation – the natural commitment and drive possessed by most people – is freed and channeled toward achievable goals.

Echoing Rabbi Menachem's strategy, Nicholson recommends applying the philosophy of judo. "Find the person's locus of energy and leverage it to achieve your ends. Instead of pushing solutions on people with the force of your argument... pull solutions out of them.

Turning the tables gets employees' attention at the very least. Ideally, it prompts them to clear the obstacles impeding their motivation."[32]

Walt Disney's film *The Lion King* contains a charming illustration of this strategy for bringing a person to reach your desired conclusion on his own[33]. The young lion Simba has fled to the jungle to escape the responsibility of succeeding his father Mufasa as king. Simba's childhood friend Nala attempts to persuade him to return by appealing to his sense of responsibility – only Simba can save the kingdom from starvation. When this argument fails to sway Simba, Nala tries guilt, telling Simba that she is disappointed to see how he has changed for the worse. Again, Simba is unmoved.

When Nala's confrontational tactics fail to bring about a change in Simba, Rafiki the baboon spiritual leader succeeds by applying a bit of transformational judo. He attracts Simba's attention by swinging deliriously from tree to tree singing strange songs. When Simba asks who he is, Rafiki turns the question around: *"The question is: Whooo... are you? ... You don't even know who you are... You're Mufasa's boy... He's alive! And I'll show him to you."*

Rafiki runs off, the pursued instead of the pursuer. When the baboon finally allows the lion to catch up with him, they are standing at a pool. Hoping to see his father, Simba looks down and sees only his own image, but Rafiki encourages him to look harder.

Simba has grown up since the last time he took a good look at his own face, and he himself perceives that his reflection now strikingly resembles his father's. At this moment of self-recognition, Rafiki delivers the message that transforms Simba's life: *"You see, he lives in you."*

Wise manager that he is, Rafiki effects change by artfully engineering Simba's "spontaneous" moment of autonomous discovery.

Chapter Summary: Lessons in Setting Objectives from the Hasidic Masters

Here is a recap of the lessons from the stories in this chapter.

Setting Strategy

- *Take the long view. Learn to cry during triumphs and laugh during disasters.* Maintain perspective beyond the moment and plan ahead for the eventualities evident to you, though not yet to others.
- *There's more than one winning strategy. If executed with total commitment, even applying leeches can be a winning strategy.* Total commitment, flawless execution and fast thinking are just as important as the choice of a plan.

Planning Change

- *There is not always a better alternative. The current situation, with all its flaws, may be the best available alternative.* Execute change only if you are convinced that it has a reasonable chance to provide clear and tangible improvements over the current situation.
- *Change what matters. Change substance, not symbols.* Make sure you are changing things that have a real impact.
- *Don't rush to judge the harmony of the grand plan.* Before you set out to change something, make sure you really understand how it works today, and make sure it really needs fixing.

Changing People

- *Change must come from within. You can't change a person — you can only make him want to change.* Using the judo approach of channeling a person's own momentum, seek to create an instant of recognition, a spontaneous discovery by the person himself of the preferable alternative.

80

CHAPTER 3

Organizing the Group

Dilbert. March 9, 2002

Rabbi Naftali of Ropshitz once told his Hasidim, "Some Rebbes pray to God that those in need of help should find salvation through the Rebbe's prayers. That is not my way. I arise early in the morning, and pray to God that all those in need may find salvation in their own homes, and not have to come to Ropshitz to ask me to pray for them."

"… a manager *organizes*. He analyzes the activities, decisions and relations needed. He classifies the work. He divides it into manageable activities. He further divides the activities into manageable jobs. He groups these units and jobs into an organization structure. He selects people for the management of these units and for the jobs to be done."[34]

- Peter F. Drucker

א

To convey his message to the world, the Rebbe gathers a group of loyal disciples around him. He chooses his followers carefully, rejects those who will not or cannot follow his ways, and grooms the most promising among them to be rebbes themselves one day. The disciples form a tight-knit group, with their own unique habits and dress, who support each other through physical and spiritual challenges.

The Rebbe strives to empower his followers. He helps them grow to the point where they can pinpoint the source of, and solve, their own problems. He doesn't do the job for them, but his guidance helps his followers to do the work themselves.

Let's see what the Hasidic masters can teach us about organizing the group: hiring and firing personnel, selecting team leaders, building teams that work together, and delegating authority to team members.

HIRING PERSONNEL

Lesson 12: Look For Committed People

Inside and Outside

The Talmud relates that when Rabbi Gamliel became the head of the Rabbinic Academy in Yavneh he was unhappy with the quality of the students. Their erudition and intellectual ability were undeniably high, but they lacked commitment and sincerity.

Rabbi Gamliel set a guard at the door of the academy and announced, "Any student whose 'inside' (character) is not the same as his 'outside' (external appearance) is barred from entering the Academy!"

When analyzing this story, Rabbi Menachem Mendel of Kotsk posed the rhetorical question, "How could the guard at the door possibly determine whether a student's inside and outside were the same? Could the guard read minds? Only God truly knows a person's inner character."

He commented, "We must therefore say that the guard, in fact, let no one through the door. Any student who climbed up the outer wall and crawled into the academy through the window – that was the sign that his inside was the same as his outside, that he was a student who truly wanted to learn."

Look For People Who Would Climb Through The Window Every Morning To Get In

A Farmer's Prayer

Zalman Pozner, who owned a large estate in Covari, was one of the rare Jews allowed to own land in nineteenth-century Eastern Europe. Hoping to improve the lot of his fellow Jews, he provided several poor Jewish families with land and equipment so that they might earn their living as farmers.

Rabbi Joshua of Kotna once visited the estate and Zalman took him on a tour of the farm. Rabbi Joshua noticed a striking difference between the fields on Zalman's estate and the fields of the neighboring Gentile farmers. On Zalman's land, shriveled crops straggled in barren furrows, while bountiful crops flourished in the verdant fields of the neighbors.

"Why are the Gentile farmers so much more successful than the Jewish farmers?" asked Rabbi Joshua.

"You can see for yourself," replied Zalman, "that the Gentile and the Jew both do the same work in the field. The Gentile plows and the Jew plows, the Gentile sows and the Jew sows, the Gentile prays and the Jew prays. The difference, I believe, is in their prayers. What does the Gentile pray for? That the rains should fall at the proper time, that the wheat should grow tall, that there should be a blessing upon the threshing floor. But what does the Jew pray for? 'Please, Lord, may it be Your will that my plow should strike buried treasure, so that I no longer need to earn my living as a farmer.'"

A Successful Team Prays Not For Buried Treasure But For Rain

Like Rabbi Gamliel, staff your team with people whose hearts are in their work and who have the determination and ingenuity to overcome obstacles. Like Zalman, you must ask yourself, "Is my team looking for ways to make the company succeed, or for a better job?" The value of having motivated employees is not theoretical – it can be measured in dollars and cents.

In Today's World

An example of the observable benefit of having motivated employees comes from the airline industry. Most airlines have dismal labor-management relations and largely dysfunctional corporate cultures.

"We don't want to kill the golden goose. We just want to choke it by the neck until it gives us every last egg," says Rick Dubinsky, head of United Airlines' pilots' union, about his approach to negotiating with management. Perhaps this adversarial stance results from bad experiences. Once at American Airlines the unions were persuaded to accept $1.62 billion in annual concessions to help the airline avoid bankruptcy, only to discover that management had just paid itself large bonuses and pensions.

What quality of service can disgruntled employees possibly provide to passengers? In such a labor- and service-intensive business, it's not surprising that most airlines are bleeding red ink.

The few airlines that are profitable – JetBlue and Southwest Airlines, for example – have one striking element in common: fierce motivation. Southwest selectively hires service-oriented employees whom they reward with generous plans for profit-sharing, stock purchase and stock options. The result is an energetic, passionate workforce whose high caliber of service wins points with customers.

Once, for example, a Southwest pilot was chatting with a young mother when she realized that her baby's bottle was in the suitcase she had checked. Looking out the window, the pilot saw the ground crew loading the suitcases onto the plane. Scrambling down the stairs to the tarmac, he followed the mother's signals until he found the right suitcase. As he climbed back into the airplane with the baby's bottle, the passengers burst into applause.[35]

One of the bestselling business books of the past few years is *Fish! A Remarkable Way to Boost Morale and Improve Results*[36], which describes the success secrets of the fishmongers at the Pike Place fish market in Seattle. Selling fish is tough work, with twelve-hour shifts, constant stench, impatient customers and inclement weather. Yet, these fishmongers turn their work into energetic play, replete with fish-tossing antics and theatrical clowning to entertain customers.

Pike Place has gung-ho employees who love their work, which translates into adoring mobs who buy their product. The same principle applies to any business. Build a team of employees who have a positive attitude, turn their work into play, and strive to engage and delight customers. Then set them loose and watch the customers roll in.

Lesson 13: Look For The Small Clues

Is He a Man at Peace?

Rabbi Israel of Rozhin once received a delegation from a nearby village. "Rabbi, we have come to complain about our town's *shochet* (ritual slaughterer). We believe he is lax in his duties, judging animals that are unfit for eating to be kosher and slaughtering animals with negligence regarding the required ordinances. We ask for your permission to dismiss him and replace him with a more stringent shochet."

Rabbi Israel listened carefully. "This is a most serious accusation," he said. "You are proposing to destroy a man's livelihood and reputation. I must investigate the matter myself before I issue a ruling." The delegation left, confident that Rabbi Israel would take their side.

Rabbi Israel looked over the Hasidim in his court for someone to act as a messenger and his eye settled on Yossi. Like many Hasidim, Yossi was not particularly learned about the intricacies of Jewish law. But he was loyal, and would follow his Rebbe's command without question.

"Yossi," said Rabbi Israel, "I would like you to travel to this village. When you arrive there, go to the shochet's home and examine his activities."

Yossi was puzzled, for he knew nothing about the laws of ritual slaughtering. He knew that a shochet must be an expert in both anatomy and Jewish law, and must maintain the highest standards of performance and integrity. A shochet would have passed a rigorous training program and acquired certification from a respected rabbi. Yossi considered himself unqualified to certify a shochet but he did not question his Rebbe's request. He took a horse and carriage and set off immediately on his journey.

It was early winter. Yossi drove through mud and driving rain, and finally arrived at the village late in the evening, cold and exhausted. A light shone from a house in the center of town, where he knocked on the door.

"C… c… can you please tell me where the shochet lives?" he stammered through chattering teeth.

"Why, I am the shochet," said the man at the door. "Please come in. You must be frozen!"

Yossi entered the shochet's home and warmed himself at the fireplace in which danced a crackling fire. The glow of candles lit the house. It seemed to Yossi that the shochet's face itself glowed with joy at the opportunity to provide hospitality to a visitor.

The shochet asked no questions about the purpose of his guest's visit and bustled about to make Yossi comfortable. He brought dry clothing and showed Yossi to a room where he could change. The shochet's wife prepared steaming tea, which Yossi drank gratefully, then laid out a meal of warm bread and hot stew. The shochet brought water and a bowl to the table so Yossi could wash his hands before eating, then used a sharp knife to cut the soft bread into thick, even slices.

When Yossi finished eating, his host told him, "You must be exhausted from your trip. Please rest." Yossi found his bed awaiting him, and soon fell asleep under a thick quilt.

When Yossi awoke in the morning, the logs in the fireplace were already burning bright. His hostess laid out a hearty meal, and the shochet reported that the weather was clearing. The shochet was too gracious to ask why Yossi had come to town, and Yossi was too embarrassed to tell the shochet that the purpose of the visit was to spy on him. After breakfast, Yossi departed, returned to Rozhin, and went straight to his Rebbe.

"Well," said Rabbi Israel, "tell me your evaluation of this shochet."

"Rebbe, I do not know a lot about slaughtering," responded Yossi. "But you told me to travel there, so I went. I arrived half-frozen from the trip. The shochet hosted me generously. His house is warm and well-lit, his hearth is crackling, his face is cheerful, his wife is hospitable. He fed me hearty meals. His bread is warm, and his knife is sharp. I slept well, arose in the morning and departed. More than this I cannot tell you."

Rabbi Israel reflected. After a few moments, he said, "I need not investigate any further. The villagers think that I will test the shochet on his knowledge of Jewish law, or that, as a Rebbe, I will look within his heart to determine whether he is God-fearing. But these examinations are meaningless – the shochet knows the laws, or he would not have received certification, and only God can see into the hearts of men. Yossi, you have given the best testimony I could desire about the shochet. His house is warm, his face cheerful, and his knife sharp – these are signs that he is still meticulous in the performance of his duties. Send a message to the villagers that their shochet is fit and may not be dismissed."

A Cheerful Face Is One Sign Of A Devoted Worker

Rabbi Israel takes a holistic approach to evaluation. A man who is content, whose house is warm and well-lit, whose family is gracious to strangers, whose knife is sharp – such a man must be in harmony with everything in his life, including his work. A man who earns his living by deceit, by passing off unkosher meat as kosher, would be nervous, fearful of being found out, too secretive to allow guests in his home. Look at any aspect of a man's life and other aspects become clear. These seemingly irrelevant clues, says Rabbi Israel, are more reliable than direct evidence, which can be hard to obtain or easily fabricated.

A manager is often called upon to evaluate people. Consider the process of interviewing a prospective new employee. Perhaps in your early days as a manager, you could grill candidates on difficult technical issues and pick out the potential stars. However, after several years as a manager, not only is it likely that your own hands-on know-how has diminished, but a candidate who reaches you has probably already passed several rounds of rigorous technical screening.

The highest value you can add to the selection process is in evaluating the intangibles, the holistic signs that surround and testify about a person. Does the candidate seem comfortable and excited about the prospect of working in your organization? Does she wince and change the subject about any aspect of her employment history? Did the prospect quit jobs or leave situations due to not getting along with others? Why? Pick up on the little signs – they are all there during the interview process.

In Today's World

I once hired a programmer with little direct experience largely because he had been captain of his high school soccer team. This struck me as an indicator of a valuable personality trait that cannot be taught: an uncompromising desire to excel. He proved me right – he quickly picked up the knowledge he lacked and became a star performer.

Many high-tech companies have moved away from traditional interview questions such as "What are your strengths and weaknesses?" to brainteasers that test problem-solving abilities. At Microsoft, for example, interviewers ask questions like "How would you move Mount Fuji?", "How do they make M&M's?", "How many piano tuners are there in the world?", "How would you design a spice rack for a blind person?", and "Why are manhole covers round?"[37] Candidates at Fog Creek Software might be asked, "How many gas stations are in Los Angeles?" or "How much does the Washington Monument weigh?"[38]

The interviewer is interested in how the candidate analyzes the problem, rather than whether she arrives at the correct answer. The goal is to identify candidates who attack difficult, unanticipated questions with logic and creativity without getting flustered. Microsoft and other hi-tech companies believe that this trait predicts future success better than does past experience.

Candidates will approach these questions differently. If you ask, "How would you move Mount Fuji?" you may get an irreverent reaction like "Where do you need it moved to?" or "Why would you want to move Mount Fuji?" Instead of disqualifying the candidate for being flip, you might decide that such an employee is valuable because she questions assumptions or thinks out of the box.

FIRING

Lesson 14: Be Aware Of The Consequences Of Firing

My Children and My Children's Children

This time, little Zalman had gone too far. He was well known as the most disruptive student in his school, and many a lesson had been ruined by his antics. Punching the boy next to him, leaving a cup of water on the teacher's chair, starting a fire outside the classroom window – Zalman had pulled these pranks and more. But in late nineteenth-century Russia, the Jewish community was committed to providing a Jewish education to all children, even unruly ones.

This morning, though, Zalman had crossed the line. Arriving early, he had gone to the school's synagogue, opened the Holy Ark where the Torah scrolls are kept, and placed a goat inside. The students assembled for morning prayers and when they opened the Ark, out sprang the bleating goat. In the ensuing chaos, the faculty quickly identified Zalman as the culprit.

His teacher dragged Zalman by the ear into the principal's office. "You must expel this child!" he demanded. "His behavior is uncontrollable, and he distracts the other students. The other teachers and I refuse to struggle with him any longer."

The principal, too, had had his fill of Zalman's disruptions, but he understood that expulsion was

93

a grave matter. There were no other Jewish schools in town, and Zalman's parents could not afford a private tutor. Out of school, Zalman would never learn even basic Jewish literacy. The principal weighed this dilemma.

"I agree with you," he replied. "But, as you know, I do not have the authority to expel a student. Only the director of Jewish education, Rabbi Shalom Baer of Lubavitch, can make such a decision. We will bring the case before him."

Rabbi Shalom, the Rebbe of the Lubavitch Hasidim, was the preeminent Jewish leader of turn-of-the-century Russia and had been appointed by the Czar to oversee all Jewish education in the realm. The principal and the teacher took Zalman with them to Lubavitch to bring the case before the Rebbe.

Rabbi Shalom listened carefully as the principal presented the litany of Zalman's misdeeds. He questioned the teacher carefully on Zalman's desecration of the Holy Ark. Although he rarely approved expulsion, Rabbi Shalom saw that, in this case, it was justified.

"You have my approval to expel the child," he announced with some reluctance.

The ensuing silence was broken, to everyone's surprise, by Zalman himself. "Rebbe, please reconsider," he pleaded. "If you expel me from school, you are not just punishing me now but for the rest of my life. You are dooming me to a life of ignorance. I will never know how to pray or to study the commandments of the Torah. And you are not just punishing me; you are punishing my children and my children's children. They will be raised by an unlearned man, and will never merit to see the light of Torah."

Zalman's words were all the more moving for being unexpected. Rabbi Shalom looked into the boy's eyes as if seeing something there for the first time. Perhaps

Zalman's logic had swayed him. Perhaps he was re-assessing the potential of a boy who understood the future consequences of today's actions.

Rabbi Shalom turned to the principal. "The boy speaks the truth. His misdeed is serious, but for his sake and the sake of his children, he deserves one more chance. His future actions will demonstrate whether he truly understands the words he has just spoken."

So Zalman returned to school. While he did not become a model student, he exercised enough self-control to complete his formal Jewish education.

Several generations later in America, Zalman's grandson married Rabbi Shalom's great-granddaughter. Not only Zalman's descendants, but also those of Rabbi Shalom himself, had Rabbi Shalom to thank for the wise decision that changed their lives.

Be Generous With Second Chances –The Consequences Can Reach Far Into The Future

Zalman's antics threaten his future and that of his children. Zalman gets another chance by changing Rabbi Shalom's perspective, and by reminding him to evaluate the consequences of punishment in both the short term and the long term.

Some of the most serious and difficult decisions you have to make as a manager involve firing people. A decision to terminate a person's employment can seriously impact his career, his self-esteem and his family life for years to come. A person's future, and that of his entire family, may hang in the balance.

In some cases it is clear that the employee is unsuited for the job, is performing poorly, or is not investing the required effort. With the stakes so high, try to emulate Rabbi Shalom and take a longer-term perspective. Can you transfer the worker to a job more suited to his strengths? Might a heart-to-heart talk about the employee's personal

95

problems show that you are sympathetic, while setting a deadline for improved performance? In short, can you find a better alternative than dismissal?

Try to exhaust all other options before resorting to dismissal. Sometimes you can find a win-win solution. Either way, when you know you have done your best to help an employee succeed, you'll find it easier to live with the consequences of firing.

In Today's World

The unprecedented success enjoyed by Jack Welch as the CEO of General Electric has made him an icon in the business world, prompting managers worldwide to emulate his leadership style. Welch earned the title "Neutron Jack," after the nuclear bomb that vaporizes people but leaves buildings standing, for his decision in the early 1980's to save the company via drastic downsizing, cutting GE by over 100,000 jobs. In retrospect, this proved to be the right move. 100,000 people joined the ranks of the unemployed, but this painful move preserved the livelihood of the remaining employees.

Welch did not stop there. Even after GE achieved financial stability, he instituted an ongoing process of firing which he calls "the Vitality Curve." Each year, every manager is required to fire those employees who perform in the bottom 10%. Companies such as Cisco, Conoco, and EDS have imitated GE in this annual ranking and elimination system. No longer a drastic but necessary response to an emergency situation, the practice of firing has become an ongoing management routine.

Critics point out that this system is counter-productive to good business:

- Poor performance might be due to other root causes – hiring the wrong person, inadequate training, flawed supervision – that firing does not identify or address.
- Fear of failure breeds mediocrity. When employees are anxious about falling into the bottom 10%, they stop taking the risks that might lead to breakthroughs.

Rather than elevating performance, a quota system tends to bunch everyone in the middle of the scale.

- After the first round or two of firing, when the truly poor performers are gone, forced firings can turn into a distracting, stressful and unnecessary war for survival among the remaining productive employees.
- It is usually more expensive to hire and train a new employee than to keep an adequate performer.
- Loyalty is a two-way street. When people see their company summarily firing loyal employees after one bad year, how long will they stick around when the company falls on hard times or the job market picks up?
- The legality of this quota system has been successfully challenged in numerous court cases.

Consider this: if the Vitality Curve had been in effect when Jack Welch was starting his career at General Electric, it's extremely likely that he would have been fired from his very first job. He was the manager of a pilot plant, responsible for everything that went on in his building. One day the building exploded in a work-related accident that shattered every window and blew off the roof.

Fearing for his job, Jack was called in to explain the explosion to a senior executive. Much to Welch's surprise, the manager was not angry, and simply asked why the accident had occurred and how to prevent such mishaps in the future. Welch claims to have learned an important first-hand lesson from this incident.

"When people make mistakes, the last thing they need is discipline. It's time for encouragement and confidence-building. The job at this point is to restore self-confidence. I think 'piling on' when someone is down is one of the worst things that any of us can do."[39] Welch was given a second chance, and his career flourished.

Now imagine what would have happened if Jack's manager had been operating under the Vitality Curve, looking to fire 10% of his workforce. Whom would he fire: a young manager who had just blown up his plant, or one who hadn't? Welch's career at GE would probably have been nipped in the bud, and GE would have been the worse for it.

Leaving aside the business considerations, Welch's Vitality Curve raises serious ethical issues. Firing people may be essential when a company is struggling to survive, but is it necessary in a thriving, successful company? As the saying goes, the only difference between surgery and sadism is the state of the patient.

Jack Welch recalls an incident in his autobiography. [40] One day, his eight-year old son John was sitting on the school bus, minding his own business, when another boy lunged at him and, for no apparent reason, punched him in the face. Jack investigated and discovered that he himself had just fired the boy's father.

Welch cites this incident as an example of the burden placed on his family by his career. Rabbi Shalom might suggest a different lesson for this story. Welch fired a man. As a result, the world became a worse place for that man, for his children, and, ultimately, for Welch and his own children as well.

SELECTING TEAM LEADERS

Lesson 15: Your Genealogy Doesn't Make You A Leader

What Makes a King?

Rabbi Israel of Rozhin, the descendant of a long and distinguished rabbinic dynasty, was once asked to explain how his lineage contributed to his greatness. He told this story.

"A prince had a loyal dog that worked hard on hunting trips and guarded his castle. The dog eventually grew old and could no longer serve his master. The prince could not bring himself to kill the dog after so many years of loyal service so he devised a plan to give the dog a chance to survive. He ordered his servants to wrap the dog in the skins of a bear, a tiger and a wolf, so that other animals would be frightened away, then instructed the servants to set the dog loose in the forest. And so the dog wandered in the forest, and all the animals feared him.

Word soon reached the lion that a new king had arrived in the forest – an animal that had the combined strength of a bear, a tiger and a wolf. The lion sent the clever fox to investigate.

'Please tell me, sir, who are you?' the fox asked the strange creature.

'My great grandfather was a bear!' the animal said with a swagger.

99

'Yes,' said the fox, 'but who are you?'

'My grandfather was a tiger!' said the creature proudly.

'Fine,' pressed the fox, 'but who are you?'

'My father was a wolf!' said the creature, a hint of defensiveness creeping into his voice.

'Clearly, but who are you?'

'I… well, I am a dog,' mumbled the creature.

With a laugh of derision, the fox ran off to tell the lion."

"So it is with distinguished lineage," said Rabbi Israel. "Having a bear, a lion or a wolf for an ancestor is meaningless if I am a dog."

> *Having A Lion In Your Family Tree Means Nothing If You Yourself Are A Dog*

There are many sources of power for a manager: the position itself, the implied backing of higher levels of management, and the ability to reward or punish. A manager uses all of these, but none of them will succeed in the long term unless the manager is genuinely worthy of the position.

In Today's World

The saga of Wang Laboratories of Lowell, Massachusetts illustrates what can happen when a company appoints a manager who is not worthy of the position. Wang Labs was founded in 1951 by An Wang, a Shanghai native who immigrated to the United States at age twenty-five. The family-run computer manufacturing company grew rapidly and, by 1984, had revenues of $2.28 billion and employed 30,000 people.

Wang insisted that his son Frederick take over the business when he decided to retire in the mid-1980's. The board of directors opposed the choice, regarding Frederick as an unqualified manager who was immature, impatient and overbearing.

"He is my son. He can do it," said Wang. This blatant nepotism caused a number of senior managers to resign, and John Cunningham, the company's most prominent non-family executive, secretly sold millions of dollars worth of his stock in the company.

Three years later, with Wang Laboratories reeling from massive losses and with 90% of its market capitalization wiped out, An Wang was forced to fire his son.

It would not be fair to blame Wang Labs' downfall entirely on Fred Wang's incompetence. Other factors, such as the emerging PC revolution and the rise of Microsoft, may have contributed. But it was a strategic blunder to appoint an unseasoned family member to head the company at such a critical juncture, and the misstep threatened the company's survival. Fred Wang's ancestry may have boasted a lion, but this did not qualify him for the job.[41]

Family-run businesses, if they manage to work around the risk of nepotism, have some major advantages. A recent *Business Week* study concluded that in one-third of the companies in the Standard & Poor Index – 177 out of 500 corporations – founders or their relatives control senior management and the board of directors. Family-run companies include the William Wrigley Jr. Co., Nordstrom, Campbell Soup, Motorola, Comcast and Cintas. Surprisingly or not, these family-run companies solidly outperform the others, with average revenue growth of 23.4% compared to 10.8% and annual shareholder return of 15.6%, compared to 11.2% for non-family-run companies.

"The family name is on the door. It's more than a job," says William Wrigley, Jr., the fourth generation CEO of his company.

Business Week concludes that family managers are far more loyal and passionate about their work than any hired hand. Family members put corporate interests before personal ones and are willing to sacrifice short-term gain for long-term growth. Tight-knit family corporations can also maneuver faster than corporate bureaucracies, acting quickly to resolve and implement major decisions.[42]

To paraphrase Rabbi Israel, perhaps the ideal leader for a company is a distinguished lion, himself the descendant of distinguished lions.

BUILDING TEAMS

Lesson 16: The Winning Team Pulls Together

They Fight as One

Napoleon's early successes in the Franco-Russian War put Jewish leaders in a delicate position. Some rabbis living under the oppression of the Czar's rule welcomed Napoleon as a savior, but others worried that the French Enlightenment would undermine the rock-solid commitment of Russian Jews to their faith. Most rabbis adopted a policy of neutrality, waiting to see which side would emerge victorious.

As Napoleon's army swept through Russia, a French general who stopped in the town of Volozhin requested a meeting with the famous Rabbi Haim of Volozhin, known far and wide among both Jews and Gentiles for his wisdom in worldly affairs. Rabbi Haim was reluctant to be drawn into a political discussion, but as an invitation from an occupying general could not be declined, Rabbi Haim went to the general's headquarters.

The two men discussed various religious matters and each was impressed with the other's erudition. Finally, the general asked Rabbi Haim, "You have a reputation for wisdom in worldly matters. Do you think the French army will defeat the Russians? Please tell me the truth."

"If it is the truth you seek," replied Rabbi Haim, "then I must tell you that I believe the Russians will win the war."

"I appreciate your honesty, Rabbi," said the general. "But as a military man, I assure you that the French forces have far superior training and equipment. Our army is made up of the finest soldiers in the French Empire. The Russian army is a ragtag band of untrained peasants."

"With your permission, I will tell you an incident that I witnessed when I was a boy," said Rabbi Haim.

"A baron's luxurious coach drawn by four powerful thoroughbred stallions sunk mired in a swamp. The coachman whipped the steeds furiously, but no matter how the horses labored, the coach did not budge.

At that moment, a local farmer happened by in a simple wagon pulled by two nags. To the baron's surprise, the farmer maneuvered his wagon around the coach and through to the other side of the swamp.

'Stop,' shouted the baron to the farmer. 'Please tell me, where did you find such remarkable horses that can traverse this mud with ease?'

The farmer laughed. 'Your Lordship, there is nothing remarkable about my nags. Your pedigreed horses are far more valuable than mine, and that is precisely your problem. Each of your horses wishes to prove to the others that it is the strongest. So, when one horse pulls, the other horses do nothing, because they do not wish to help the other horse succeed. My poor nags may have no pedigree, but they grew up together and when they pull the wagon it is a joint endeavor.'"

"With all due respect, General," continued Rabbi Haim, "I believe this is the problem of your army. Your soldiers are well trained and have excellent pedigrees, but they come from diverse backgrounds and each soldier fights strictly for his own glory. Not so the

Russian army. They are all one nationality, and each member fights for a common cause – their homeland. They fight as one. This is why I believe that the Russian army will win the war."

The ensuing years proved Rabbi Haim's assessment to be correct.

The Winning Team May Not Be Pedigreed – But It Pulls Together

R abbi Haim knows what it takes to build a winning team. A group rarely fails due to a lack of talent. Often there is too much of the same kind of talent, but not enough cooperation among the team members.

Staffing your team with superstar individual performers is not the formula for success. A productive team pulls together because each member truly wants the others to succeed, and is willing to help in any way possible.

In Today's World

For nine months in 1942, the United States Navy suffered a catastrophe known as the Eastern Pearl Harbor. German U-boats operating off the Atlantic coast sunk US merchant ships at will, paralyzing America's maritime transportation. The British were far more successful in defending their ships against U-boat attack and passed on to the Americans everything they knew about sonar, depth charges and destroyers. But it was to no avail – the US Navy was unable to stop the U-boat threat.

Were they less talented than their British counterparts? On the contrary – the US Navy's Chief of Naval Operations, Ernest Joseph King, prided himself on his ability to recruit the best people and let them manage themselves. The Navy had plenty of talent at the top. What they didn't have was an organization that worked well together.

Unfortunately, that was precisely what the anti-submarine war required. The British excelled at the task because they had a centralized operational system. Analysts synthesized fragments of information into a cohesive picture that enabled controllers to coordinate the movement of warships, aircraft and merchant convoys. By contrast, throughout 1942, the US Navy stubbornly refused to learn operational lessons from the British, relying instead on technical know-how and individual effort.

Only after the Navy formed the Tenth Fleet in May of 1943 did the situation improve. The Tenth Fleet succeeded because it provided an organizational structure that enabled and encouraged people to pull together to achieve a common goal.[43]

I once took over a team of twelve engineers whose previous manager had supervised all twelve of them directly, but had promised each and every one a promotion to group leader. I devoted my first day on the job to meeting with each engineer individually.

Irene, a senior team member, spent her hour describing the failings of her colleague Stan. I left the meeting convinced that, despite her seniority and technical expertise, I could not, in good conscience, allow her to manage a junior engineer.

My next talk, with Stan, was more of the same. He related anecdotes about Irene's failings as an engineer and as a human being. He boasted of the technical problems he had solved single-handedly. I walked away convinced that he was an important individual contributor, but I saw in him more ego than management skills.

Next up was Mary, a junior engineer. I asked her to tell me about an accomplishment she was proud of. She told me about how she had successfully absorbed a new member into the team and brought him up to speed. Although Mary was not the top expert on the company's products, she was competent and enjoyed mentoring and sharing information.

That evening, mulling over these discussions, I tried to formulate what I was looking for in a group leader. It wasn't superlative engineering skills, although technical competence was a must. I decided on a rule of thumb: a group leader must be someone who enjoys building people up rather than tearing them down. That's the kind of person I want to manage me, and that's the kind of manager I trust to mentor a new employee.

A couple of weeks later, Irene was flattered when her previous boss asked her to join him in Sales, and Stan was pleased when I promoted him to Chief Technology Officer for the group with solo responsibility for solving thorny problems. With the way now clear, I promoted Mary to group leader, a role she performed with great success.

Lesson 17: The Difference Is In How People Treat Each Other

Heaven or Hell

Rabbi Haim of Romshishok was an itinerant preacher. He traveled from town to town delivering religious sermons that stressed the importance of respect for one's fellow man. He often began his talks with the following story:

"I once ascended to the firmaments. I first went to see Hell and the sight was horrifying. Row after row of tables was laden with platters of sumptuous food, yet the people seated around the tables were pale and emaciated, moaning in hunger. As I came closer, I understood their predicament. Every person held a full spoon, but both arms were splinted with wooden slats so he could not bend either elbow to bring the food to his mouth. It broke my heart to hear the tortured groans of these poor people as they held their food so near but could not consume it.

Next I went to visit Heaven. I was surprised to see the same setting I had witnessed in Hell – row after row of long tables laden with food. But in contrast to Hell, the people here in Heaven were sitting contentedly talking with each other, obviously sated from their sumptuous meal. As I came closer, I was amazed to discover that here, too, each person had his arms splinted on wooden slats that prevented him from bending his elbows. How, then, did they manage to eat?

As I watched, a man picked up his spoon and dug it into the dish before him. Then he stretched across the table and fed the person across from him! The recipient of this kindness thanked him and returned the favor by leaning across the table to feed his benefactor.

I suddenly understood. Heaven and Hell offer the same circumstances and conditions. The critical difference is in the way the people treat each other.

I ran back to Hell to share this solution with the poor souls trapped there. I whispered in the ear of one starving man, 'You do not have to go hungry. Use your spoon to feed your neighbor, and he will surely return the favor and feed you.'

'You expect me to feed the detestable man sitting across the table?' said the man angrily. 'I would rather starve than give him the pleasure of eating!'

I then understood God's wisdom in choosing who is worthy to go to Heaven and who deserves to go to Hell."

The Difference Between Heaven And Hell Is Not The Setting – It's In The Way People Treat Each Other

Rabbi Haim's parable applies as much to the corporate environment as to any other social setting. Companies all start with the same basic circumstances and conditions. Yet some companies are heaven to work in, while others are sheer hell. The difference, as Rabbi Haim astutely points out, lies in how the people treat each other. If employees cooperate and seek to help each other succeed, then coming to work every day is a pleasure. If, on the other hand, they lack respect for each other's abilities and spend their time looking for ways to shift blame, no one will enjoy showing up for work. As Luciano de Crescenzo observed, "We are all angels with only one wing; we can only fly while embracing one another."

Most people will readily recite for you the list of fellow employees and injustices making their lives miserable at work. But ask them about how they may have contributed to the pollution of the atmosphere at work, and you will get only blank stares in return. They see clearly how they suffer from a hellish environment, but not how they contribute to creating it, how their own attitudes and behavior may help create someone else's hell.

There are no managers in Rabbi Haim's firmament – each person chooses his own mode of behavior. So where do the managers belong – in Heaven or Hell?

That, of course, depends on the manager. Some encourage an atmosphere of cooperation and trust, while others foster back-biting and blame-shifting. Either way, a manager helps shape the organization's atmosphere through words and gestures, reward and punishment, and decisions on hiring and firing. In many cases, the only difference between Heaven and Hell is the manager. The right manager can transform a hellish work environment into a heaven.

In Today's World

Psychologists Richard Wagner and Robert Sternberg have developed tests that predict managerial success. Here is a question from one of their tests:

> You have just been promoted to head of an important department in your organization. The previous head has been transferred to an equivalent position in a less important department. Your understanding of the reason for the move is that the performance of the department as a whole has been mediocre. There have not been any glaring deficiencies, just a perception of the department as so-so rather than very good. Your charge is to shape up the department. Results are

expected quickly. Rate the quality of the following strategies for succeeding at your new position:

a) Always delegate to the most junior person who can be trusted with the task.
b) Give your superiors frequent progress reports.
c) Announce a major reorganization of the department that includes getting rid of whomever you believe to be "dead wood."
d) Concentrate more on your people than on the tasks to be done.
e) Make people feel completely responsible for their work.

Wagner and Sternberg find that good managers tend to pick (b) and (e), i.e., they would target communication and empowerment, while poor managers tend to pick (c), replacing team members. A good manager knows that the very same people that make up an under-performing team can, with the right motivation and communication, become a winning team. To paraphrase Rabbi Haim: there is no difference as far as the setting or the circumstances. The only difference is the way the people act towards each other.

The press tends to revere macho bosses who rely on fear and intimidation in the workplace. *Fortune* magazine regularly publishes a list of the toughest bosses. Frank Lorenzo, whose unrelenting fights with employees and unions destroyed Eastern Airlines, was hailed by the business press as a genius. When Al Dunlap, nicknamed "Chainsaw Al" for his massive layoffs at Scott Paper, was named CEO of Sunbeam, the press applauded the move and Sunbeam's stock price rose by 60%.

But results prove that management based on fear and intimidation ultimately does not work. It discourages necessary communication, demoralizes employees and drives the best people out of the organization. Dunlap was fired from Sunbeam after a massive accounting fraud, and Lorenzo lost his job at Continental Airlines because of his "scorched earth" policy towards employees.

The evidence is indisputable – companies that put their employees first and create a positive work environment outperform those that don't. To cite one study, the "100 Best Companies to Work for in America," selected for their favorable treatment of employees by *Fortune* magazine, also outperformed the Standard & Poor 500 Index by 12% and yielded higher return to shareholders over a three year period than the broad-market Russell 3000 Index.[44]

Lesson 18: Behavior Is More Important Than Beliefs

The Secret

Once in a remote Polish town, a Hasid named Yossel went mad. He was convinced that the mayor of his city was none other than the Messiah himself. With each passing day he became more obsessed with this notion and could speak of nothing else. The members of his family knew that his condition was deteriorating, and, in desperation, took him to his Rebbe, Rabbi Meir of Premishlan.

"Rebbe, the Messiah lives in my town!" blurted Yossel.

Rabbi Meir looked at the man with compassion. "What does he do there?"

"Why, he is the mayor!"

Rabbi Meir saw that Yossel spoke with utter conviction.

"Tell me," Rabbi Meir asked Yossel, "do you know who I am?"

"Why, of course," said the Hasid. "You are Rabbi Meir, the greatest Rebbe of the generation."

"If so," responded Rabbi Meir, "do you believe it possible that a holy Rebbe like myself would not know that the Messiah is in your town?"

Yossel was puzzled for a moment, then a smile spread across his face. "Of course you know all about it. But you wish to keep the Messiah's presence a secret until the time is right."

Rabbi Meir leaned close to Yossel, and whispered to him, "Well, if I can keep a secret, so can you."

From that day forward Yossel was cured. He never spoke about the matter again.

Focus On Behavior, Not Beliefs

You may feel uncomfortable with this story because it appears to encourage deceit. But take a closer look. Rabbi Meir aspires to help someone who holds such a deeply entrenched view that he is beyond reason. Rather than trying to change his belief, which would be a waste of time and energy, the wise leader sets about changing that person's behavior. If Rabbi Meir were a psychologist, we would say that he is a behaviorist. The outcome of his treatment is a well-functioning person whose behavior is normal, though his beliefs are not.

As a manager, part of your job is building consensus among subordinates and superiors. You may not agree with the beliefs of the people you work with, and some of them may be socially dysfunctional. Perhaps you would not choose your co-workers as friends. But for the good of the organization, you need to find a way to work productively with them.

In Today's World

I once worked in close partnership with an engineer named Jack. I was developing software utilities, and Jack was developing the application that used them.

Jack was a survivalist who spent his weekends building an underground home that would enable him to weather the impending world war. His wife was adept at re-assembling jeep transmissions, an important post-nuclear-holocaust skill. Frankly, Jack scared the living daylights out of me.

Our manager gave me this advice: "When you talk with Jack, stick to the task at hand. Don't get into politics." It worked. Today Jack may be living in his bomb shelter, mailing out anthrax, but at the time we were able to cooperate, odd couple though we were.

Rick Barry was a talented basketball player whose insulting comments and egotistical behavior alienated him from his teammates and impeded his professional success.

In a preseason practice game during the 1974 season, Barry so offended teammates on the Golden State Warriors with a racist remark that they plotted revenge. Clifford Ray, the team's center, beseeched his teammates to ignore Barry's off-court attitude and concentrate on how he could help the team.

"Look, Rick is harmless. Whatever he says, don't take it to heart. He doesn't mean anything by it. He just wants to win, and he can help us win."

Ray convinced the team, and the Warriors went on to sweep the Washington Bullets for the NBA title. They won despite the fact that Rick Barry himself hadn't changed. Several years later, he was fired from a sportscaster job for making an on-air racial slur.

Differences in belief can actually have a beneficial effect at work, according to researcher Debra Meyerson. She identifies a group she calls "tempered radicals," successful workers within the organization who quietly challenge its values. Rather than assimilating away their differences or leaving because of them, these employees take a middle road, constantly balancing between conformity and rebellion via a spectrum of moderate responses. This group effects gradual change, introduces practices that meet unaddressed needs, and forces organizations to question convention and examine issues from different perspectives.

Myerson offers several examples of the types of change that have been catalyzed by tempered radicals. For example, Martha Wiley grants her employees flexible work hours, despite the absence of a corporate policy to back her up. This decision pushes the organization to recognize that a growing sector of the workforce cannot function effectively in a traditional nine-to-five regime. Alan Levy's observance of Jewish holidays raises the issue of creating a calendar and holiday policy that is more sensitive to the culturally diverse workforce of his company. Peter Grant's personal efforts, over the course of a long career, to hire and mentor employees of color built a large network of minority professionals in his organization.[45]

Lesson 19: Someone Else May Help To Complete Your Idea

Finding the Hidden Treasure

In the city of Cracow there lived a Jew named Isaac Jacobs, a simple man who earned a meager but honest living by the sweat of his brow.

One night in a dream an old man with a kind face came to him and said, "God wishes to grant you wealth so that you may do good deeds. Go to Prague and dig under the base of the Royal Bridge. There you will find a treasure." When Isaac awoke he dismissed his dream as nonsense. But the dream recurred, night after night, until Isaac could no longer ignore it.

"It must be a message from Heaven," he decided, "and if God wishes to tell me something, it would be a sin to ignore Him." So Isaac Jacobs set out for Prague.

Finding the Royal Bridge was easy enough. But digging there was a different story. The area was heavily guarded, and Isaac did not see how he could possibly approach the base of the bridge, let alone start digging there, without being arrested. But Isaac believed his dream was a divine message that could not be ignored.

So Isaac took a shovel, slipped by the soldiers guarding the bridge, and began to dig. The noise attracted the attention of the captain of the guard, who went to investigate. Imagine his surprise to discover a Jew digging in the dark!

117

"What are you doing here?" he barked to Isaac at gunpoint. "Are you a spy sent against our King? Tell me quickly, or I will kill you!"

Isaac stammered, "Please, sir, I mean the King no harm. I have been having the same dream, night after night, telling me that if I dig at the base of the Royal Bridge in Prague, I will find a great treasure. I believe this dream to be a message from God, so I have traveled here to dig.... "

"You pathetic fool!" snorted the soldier. "I have never seen such a simpleton in my life. Everyone knows that dreams are sheer nonsense. Why, I myself have had strange dreams lately. An old man keeps telling me to go to Cracow, to the home of someone named Isaac Jacobs, and dig up a treasure buried beneath his stove. But I am not a fool like you. You don't see me traveling to Cracow just because I had a meaningless dream! You poor deluded wretch, I am going to release you out of pity. Leave and do not come back. And stop chasing after dreams."

Isaac Jacobs thanked the guard and hurried away. He now understood why the old man in his dream had sent him to Prague – to hear the dream of the captain of the guard. The treasure he was seeking was in his own home! He returned to Cracow and dug under the stove of his house where, indeed, he found a great treasure. From then on, Isaac was a wealthy man, and used his money to help the Jewish community of Cracow.

To Realize Dreams, Share Them

This charming story illustrates the benefits of brainstorming and teamwork. Isaac Jacobs doesn't have all the information he needs – all he has is the first step of a plan. But he is willing to get started on his plan by traveling to Prague. More important, he is willing to discuss his idea with the captain and as a result obtains the information he needs to implement his idea. In contrast, the captain is quick to dismiss his dream as nonsense, and, as a result, misses out on his own share of the treasure.

Managers can use the same process in brainstorming sessions. Encourage your team to raise all their ideas. To remove inhibitions and self-censorship that would dampen creative thinking, set ground rules: no idea is too ridiculous to raise, and no one is allowed to criticize anyone else's proposal. After all the suggestions are on the table, have the team begin to evaluate and combine ideas and converge on the solution that is most effective. Often, one person has the germ of a successful idea, and only requires information from others to make that idea feasible.

In Today's World

The invention of Post-It Notes illustrates how two ideas can combine to fulfill a dream. In 1968, Dr. Spence Silver, a research scientist for 3M Corporation, invented an adhesive with unusual properties. Each individual sphere of the substance was very sticky, but the spheres made only intermittent contact with other surfaces. As Silver explained in his information-sharing seminars, the result – a not-very-sticky adhesive – was interesting and different, but he considered it useless.

In 1974 Art Fry, a 3M researcher who had attended one of Silver's seminars six years earlier, was having an annoying problem with the hymn book at his St. Paul, Minnesota choir. Fry's bookmarks fell out between services, leaving Fry scrambling for the right place during performances. Remembering the "unglue," Fry went to the lab and applied some of the semi-sticky substance to the edge of a paper strip. To his delight, the result provided an ideal solution – a bookmark that would stay in place when needed but could be easily removed afterwards.

Fry tried for years to convince his managers of the value of this new product, but they remained skeptical. Finally in 1977 they agreed to

119

perform an internal market trial. 3M secretaries were given blocks of the glue-edged paper without any specific instructions as to what to do with them. The secretaries came up with more uses for these little yellow notes than anyone had dreamed possible, and they asked to keep the notes once the trial was over. By 1990 Post-it Notes was one of the five top-selling office supply products in America.

The invention of public key encryption is an example of brainstorming among teams separated by time and space. Cryptographers had for centuries searched for a way to set up secure communication between two people who have never met. In 1976, Whitfield Diffie and Martin Hellman from Stanford University discovered that another researcher, Ralph Merkle from the University of California at Berkeley, was working on the same problem. They realized there was synergy between their approaches and combined forces.

In Hellman's words, "We each had a key part of the puzzle and while it's true one of us first said X, and another of us first said Y, and so on, it was the combination and the back-and-forth between us that allowed the discovery."

The team published a revolutionary paper in 1976 that outlined a solution and contained sample mathematical formulas. Recognizing that their formulas provided only a partial solution, they closed their paper with an invitation to other researchers, regardless of their credentials, to contribute more useful formulas. Their guiding principle was that "Innovation, particularly in the design of new types of cryptographic systems, has come primarily from amateurs."

In 1977, inspired by the Diffie-Hellman-Merkle paper, Ronald L. Rivest, Adi Shamir and Leonard M. Adleman took up the challenge and identified a practical method to implement the encryption system. Public key encryption was born, thanks to the combined effort of remote teams who cooperated to solve a previously unsolvable problem.[46]

DELEGATING AUTHORITY

Lesson 20: Trust Your Team For The Little Things

Trust for the Penny

A woman once came to Rabbi Mordechai of Chernobyl. "I suspect that my husband is withholding money from the family," she said. "He owns a tailor shop in town, and whenever I visit, the store is full of customers. Yet at the end of the week, he barely brings home enough money to feed and clothe the children."

"Listen and I will tell you a story," said Rabbi Mordechai. "Once there was a young man who earned his living as a teacher. He traveled to remote towns and taught Jewish children to read and write. He was frugal and worked hard. After three years, he had saved twelve bags of gold coins and he decided to return to his home. He collected the fee for his last teaching assignment, a copper penny, and placed it in one of the bags, then set out on the long journey home.

The man realized on Friday afternoon that he would not reach home before the Sabbath. Fortunately he happened upon an inn and decided to stay there until Sunday morning.

As the Sabbath approached, the man was faced with a dilemma – what to do with his money? He could not carry it around with him, for handling money is forbidden on the Sabbath. Should he hide it in his room? What if one of the other guests was a thief? Should he ask the owner of the inn to guard the gold for him? What if the innkeeper was a dishonest fellow, who would later deny all knowledge of the bags of gold?

The time for the Sabbath had almost arrived and the teacher was wracked with indecision. At the last possible moment, he ran to the innkeeper's office.

'Please guard these bags for me,' he blurted. 'I will come to get them from you after the Sabbath.'

The man's decision brought him no rest. He did not sleep all that night, and felt his heart pounding all through the Sabbath. Would the innkeeper return his money?

At the conclusion of the Sabbath, the man ran to the office and asked for his bags. He counted them and breathed a sigh of relief to find all twelve. Then, to the innkeeper's surprise, the teacher opened the bags one by one, searching through their contents.

'What are you looking for?' asked the innkeeper.

'There was a copper penny in one of the bags. I am checking that it was returned along with everything else.'

'You fool!' said the innkeeper, doubled over with laughter. 'You know that I have returned all your bags of gold to you, but you suspect me of stealing a mere penny?'"

Rabbi Mordechai smiled at the woman. "Do you see? You are being as foolish as the man in the story. You entrust your husband with what you value most – you trust him to educate your children and to be an example to them. Will you not trust him to provide you with your livelihood? If you trust him each day with your children, then surely you can trust him to do something as simple as provide you with sustenance."

If You Trust Someone With Your Gold, Trust Him With Your Pennies

Rabbi Mordechai touches upon an important human trait. Like the teacher in his story and the concerned wife, we sometimes find it easier to trust people for the big things than for the little things. Perhaps it's because we understand and believe we can control the little things, like tracking money, more than we understand the big things, like raising children. Still, the innkeeper's derision is justified. Someone who is trusted with a precious treasure should certainly also be trusted for pennies.

As a manager, you trust your team for the big things – to produce the product, to represent the company, to keep corporate secrets. Your own success as a manager is in their hands. Do you also trust them for the little things, like ordering professional books or keeping track of their own time? People appreciate being trusted, and will respond by acting honorably. If you nickel-and-dime your employees on trivial issues while you assume their good faith on the big ones, you may find your team laughing at the absurdity, or, worse, violating your trust regarding the issues that matter to you most.

In Today's World

The Ritz-Carlton gives each employee $2000 of discretionary funds which s/he may use to solve a customer service problem. This is in line with the Ritz-Carlton mission statement, "We are ladies and gentlemen serving ladies and gentlemen."

The management of Nordstrom gives its employees the freedom to make decisions and is willing to live with their choices. For example, a customer once fell in love with a pair of slacks that were on sale. Unfortunately, the store was out of her size and the Nordstrom sales

123

associate was unable to locate a pair in the inventory of any other Nordstrom store. Undeterred, the associate took some petty cash from her department manager, crossed the street to a competitor's store, and bought the slacks at full price. She returned to her customer and sold her the slacks for the marked-down sale price.

Bill Hewlett, the co-founder of Hewlett-Packard, once found the door to the supply room locked. Outraged at the implied lack of trust for employees, Hewlett snapped the lock open with bolt cutters, and left a note reading, "Don't ever lock this door again."

A number of thriving companies, such as Whole Food Markets, Southwest Airlines, The Men's Wearhouse and AES Corporation, have built a culture based on trusting employees. Whole Foods, for example, which has grown to over $1 billion in sales, shares detailed financial information (including data about individual salaries by name) with all its employees, to such an extent that all employees are considered insiders by the Securities and Exchange Commission.

John Mackey, Whole Foods' CEO, explains that "to keep secrets implies that the organization doesn't trust those from whom the information is withheld. This is the wrong message to send if you want to harness the efforts and energy of everyone."[47]

Chapter Summary: Lessons in Organizing the Group from the Hasidic Masters

Here is a recap of the lessons from the stories in this chapter.

Hiring Personnel

- Look for committed people. Staff your team with people who want to be there and who have the determination to get past obstacles. *Look for people who would climb through the window every morning to get in.*
- Ask yourself, "Is my team praying for the company's success or are they praying for a better job?" *A successful team prays not for buried treasure but for rain.*
- Look for the small clues. When interviewing, evaluate the intangibles, the holistic picture that gives valuable testimony about a candidate. *A cheerful face is one sign of a devoted worker.*

Firing

- Your decision to terminate someone's employment can seriously impact his career, his self-esteem and his family life for many years to come. *Be generous with second chances. The consequences can reach far into the future.*

Selecting Team Leaders

- A manager has many sources of power, but none will succeed in the long run unless the manager is truly worthy of the position. *Having a lion in your family tree means nothing if you yourself are a dog.*

Building Teams

- A productive group does not need superstar individual performers – it needs each member to truly want the others to succeed. *The winning team may not be pedigreed – but it pulls together.*
- The quality of the work environment depends largely on how team members relate to their colleagues. *The difference between heaven and hell is not the setting – it's in the way the people treat each other.*
- Build consensus among people even if they differ radically in personality and background. *Focus on behavior, not beliefs.*
- *To realize dreams, share them.* Often, by pooling information, a team can develop a good idea into a feasible plan.

Delegating Authority

- As a manager, you trust your team for the big things – to create a product, to represent the company, to keep corporate secrets. Do you also trust them for the little things? *If you trust someone with your gold, trust him with your pennies.*

126

CHAPTER 4

Measuring Performance

A Hasid came before Rabbi Yitzchak Meir of Ger, and told of his frustration. "I have worshipped God for many years, yet I feel no progress. My prayer today is the same as my prayer twenty years ago, with no more intensity or devotion."

Rabbi Yitzchak replied, "Elijah the Prophet taught, 'Man should take the Bible upon himself as the ox takes the yoke.' You see, the ox leaves his stall every morning, puts on the yoke and plows the field, then goes home in the evening. This happens day after day, and nothing ever changes for the ox. But the ploughed field yields the harvest, and that is the true measure of the ox's progress."

"The fourth basic element in the work of a manager is *the job of measurement.* The manager establishes measuring yardsticks — and there are few factors that are as important to the organization and to every man in it. He sees to it that each man in the organization has measurements available to him which are focused on the performance of the whole organization and which at the same time focus on the work of the individual and help him do it. He analyzes performance, appraises it and interprets it. And again, as in every other area of work, he communicates both the meaning of the measurements and their findings to his subordinates as well as to his superiors."[48]

- Peter F. Drucker

א

Judaism seeks to harness boundless spiritual rapture into a defined regimen that gives structure to all aspects of human behavior, down to the smallest detail. In prayer, for example, a Jew seeks to converse with the infinite God, within a structured legal framework that precisely spells out texts and timeframes.

The Hasidic Rebbe accepts the validity of these structures, but these are not his message to the world. Rather, the Rebbe seeks to augment and extend the boundaries of Judaism to include even those that do not strictly fit within the letter of the law. While the Rebbe recognizes the importance of measurement, he looks beyond the surface to measure things that others overlook, and struggles to achieve recognition and appreciation for things that are impossible to measure.

Drucker's emphasis on measurement has become a basic tenet of modern management. Today, a manager is inundated with measurements that guide his decisions: measurements of employee performance, adherence to schedules, cost variance, sales targets, and so on. The Hasidic Rebbes teach us to look beyond the obvious, to measure that which may be difficult to observe or quantify.

Let's see what we can learn from the Hasidic Rabbis about what and how to measure: monitoring schedules, the role of measurement in managing people, and evaluating performance.

MONITORING SCHEDULES

Lesson 21: Tolerate Lateness If It Improves The Result

Why Are You Late?

Rabbi Naftali of Ropshitz knew that Jewish law defines strict timeframes for daily prayers. For example, the morning prayer must be completed within three hours after sunrise. But he was known to deviate from this schedule, and would often complete his morning prayers well after mid-day.

One afternoon, when Rabbi Naftali was in the study hall, he saw a Hasid rush in. The Hasid ran to his seat, threw on his prayer shawl, wrapped the leather straps of his tefilin (prayer phylacteries) around his arm and head, and hurried through the morning prayer. He finished within a few minutes.

"You are wrong to pray the morning prayer so late," Rabbi Naftali told the Hasid.

The Hasid stammered, "But, Rabbi, you also pray late in the day!"

"Let me tell you a story," said Rabbi Naftali. "Once there was a man whose morning schedule was constant. Every morning he rose early and went to the synagogue for the morning prayer. When he returned home, his wife prepared for him a simple meal of brown bread and raw vegetables.

One morning, when he returned from the synagogue, the table was bare.

'You must wait,' his wife told him, 'for I have not yet prepared your meal.' The man waited for an hour, then a second hour, then a third hour. Each time he asked his wife, she told him, 'Please wait – I am still preparing your meal.'

'My wife must be preparing a very special meal for me, if it is taking her so long to prepare it,' thought the man in anticipation.

The man waited and waited. Finally, after mid-day, his wife set the table and brought out the meal – brown bread and raw vegetables! The man was furious.

'After waiting so long for this meal, I expected a feast, with fish and meats and all sorts of delicacies. You could have served me the usual brown bread and raw vegetables as soon as I returned from the synagogue!'"

Rabbi Naftali continued, "The Rabbis of the generation are late in their morning prayers because they labor many hours to deliver to God a prayer with devotion, sincerity and enthusiasm. When their prayers finally arrive before God, He savors them even though they are late, for He understands that it takes time to create such a delicacy. But, a prayer such as yours, rushed and mechanical – well, such a coarse prayer could just as well have been served to God first thing in the morning!"

If You're Going To Be Late, You'd Better Serve Up A Delicacy

Timeliness is important in business, both with customers (e.g., delivering a product on time) and with employees (e.g., starting meetings on time). The moral of this story: on-time delivery is not the be-all and the end-all; sometimes lateness is acceptable. But if you're going to miss a deadline, you'd better have a persuasive reason, such as an improved end product. If the product is late but great, the customer will quickly forget a minor delay. But if the product is late and doesn't work – to paraphrase Rabbi Naftali, such a product could just as well have been delivered on time.

In Today's World

A recent survey of Information Technology executives by software company Compuware SA reached some interesting conclusions about the importance of on-time delivery. 31% of the executives in the study said their main objective was to ensure that software development projects were delivered on time, versus only 23% who said their primary aim was to ensure that the application had the features needed to meet the customer's business needs.

Compuware sales manager Graeme Allcock concludes from this data, "The metric these executives use to determine whether an application meets quality targets is not whether it meets business requirements but whether it's delivered on time.... These responses are concerning. It seems that when it comes down to practicalities, quality has to take a back seat to the delivery imperative."[49]

There may be other conclusions we can draw from this data, as almost half of those surveyed named other factors besides timeliness or quality as their main criteria for success, and in any case, according to a Standish Group study, only 16.2% of Information Technology projects are considered successful by customers. In delivering a product of this type, you will boost the chances of satisfying your customer if you determine, in advance, the client's main criteria for success.

Management expert Jim Collins describes the Silicon Valley Paradigm for businesses: start with a great idea, raise money from venture capitalists, grow rapidly, go public, and generate wealth for the investors as quickly as possible. According to Collins, this "beat the clock" mentality results in one-product companies that briefly fly high and then crash, rather than great companies that will endure over time.

The corporate landscape is littered with companies whose stars shone brightly, then burnt out because they were really products, not companies. Look at Software Arts (makers of the first spreadsheet), Osbourne Computer (producers of the first portable computer), Ashton-Tate (developers of the first PC database), and, more recently, Netscape (developer of the first commercial Web browser).

In contrast, the great companies that survive and thrive over time – Motorola, Hewlett-Packard, Sony, General Motors, 3M, Disney – started with a different paradigm. They defined their missions more broadly and, typically, grew slowly, their attention focused on building a great company, rather than on one initial great product. They invested time and effort in laying the foundation and determining their core values. They took the time to develop an ongoing organizational ability to come up with great products, to take those products to market, to provide customers with outstanding service, and all the other skills required to succeed on an ongoing basis.

This long-term, patient view seems to be far more successful than the Silicon Valley Paradigm in building great companies than last.[50]

MEASUREMENT AND MANAGEMENT

Lesson 22: Measurement Is Not A Substitute For Management

Like a Tree

The Bible states, in Deuteronomy 20:19, "… for man is like the tree of the field."

"How is man like a tree?" asked Rabbi Uri of Strelisk. "I will explain by way of a story."

"Once there was a man who desired to see how a tree grows. So he positioned himself in front of the tree and sat there for many days, hoping to catch a glimpse of growth.

One day a traveler passed and saw the man gazing at the tree. 'What are you doing?' asked the traveler.

'I am trying to see how much this tree has grown,' replied the man. 'But I don't see any progress!'

'You are going about it all wrong!' laughed the traveler. 'If you watch the tree incessantly and only measure its growth, you will see nothing at all. But if you cultivate the tree – give it water, prune it in the proper season, protect it from harmful pests – then, in good time, it will grow, and you will merit to see its growth.'"

"The same is true of a man," taught Rabbi Uri. "Provide him with the nourishment and nurturing he requires, and he will surely thrive. But if you examine him at every hour to see how much he has grown, you will not see any growth, for there will be none."

Don't Just Measure – Nurture

This story describes the delicate balance a manager must strike between measuring performance and micromanaging. Rabbi Uri does not suggest that we do away with measurement entirely. Measuring achievement provides the employee with a sense of accomplishment and gives the manager valuable feedback on the effectiveness of his 'tending.' But Rabbi Uri teaches us that incessant measurement can have a harmful effect when it is the manager's main preoccupation and replaces the real work of management – providing mentoring, motivation and support.

In Today's World

There are two fundamental approaches to managing people, maintains Douglas McGregor in his book *The Human Side of Enterprise*[51]. Theory X managers use an authoritarian management style, and Theory Y managers implement a participative management style.

A Theory X manager assumes that the average employee seeks to avoid responsibility, prefers to be directed, dislikes work and will avoid it if possible, and has relatively little ambition. To manage such employees, the Theory X manager sees his role as coercing and controlling workers, issuing deadlines and ultimatums, and focusing on short-term results rather than future improvements.

A Theory Y manager, by contrast, believes that work is as natural as play and rest. People have potential and, once they are committed to objectives, they want to exercise self-direction and responsibility to fulfill it. A Theory Y manager therefore sees his role as developing the potential that is inherent in employees and helping them to release that potential toward a common goal.

135

McGregor maintains that far too many managers tend toward Theory X and therefore generally get poor results, while enlightened managers use Theory Y, which produces better long-term performance and results.

Like all Hasidic Rebbes, Rabbi Uri is a Type Y manager who believes that his role is not primarily to measure his followers, but first and foremost to provide them with the proper conditions so that they can thrive.

א

From 1924 to 1932, Harvard Business School professor Elton Mayo studied ways to improve productivity at Western Electric's Hawthorne plant near Chicago. The first experiment measured the effect of improving the lighting in the work area of a team of women who inspected parts and assembled relays.

Initial results were promising – installing brighter lighting significantly increased the team's productivity. But then an investigator decided to repeat the study with decreased lighting, and found that this also improved productivity! It was not the increased lighting that had improved performance – merely performing an experiment and showing interest in the factory workers spurred them on to improved job performance.

This phenomenon has come to be known as The Hawthorne Effect: measuring something in a work situation inevitably causes a short-term improvement in whatever is being observed, though there may be no other reason for improvement, as employees try to guarantee that the measurement will reflect favorably on them.

The Hawthorne Theory proves Rabbi Uri's point: give employees even the most meager nourishment – the attention that comes with being measured – and watch them grow. It also adds a corollary to Rabbi Uri's teaching: when measuring people and not trees, mere measurement may indeed appear to produce some improvement, but it will be limited and short-term.

EVALUATING PERFORMANCE

Lesson 23: Look Beyond The Insult

Mendelsohn's Recommendation

Hasidism was by no means the only Jewish revolution of its time. In the nineteenth century, the Reform movement swept through Western Europe, encouraging Jews to relax the strictures of Jewish law. Hasidim and other Orthodox groups united to oppose these reforms, and many Jewish communities were torn apart by the resulting controversy.

In Hamburg, both Reform and Orthodox Jews sat on the council that oversaw Jewish communal affairs. When the Chief Rabbi of Hamburg passed away, this council had to find a candidate that was acceptable to both sides.

Finally, after months of argument, the council interviewed Rabbi Raphael Hacohen. He impressed the Orthodox representatives with his Talmudic erudition and his commitment to Jewish tradition. The Reformers were impressed with Rabbi Raphael's openness to secular culture, but were concerned that he had never had any direct contact with the Reform movement.

"Let us send him to Berlin to meet with the leader of German Reform, Moses Mendelsohn," suggested the leader of the council. "The Reformers on our council all respect Mendelsohn's opinion." So the Hamburg council sent a letter to Mendelsohn, requesting his help in evaluating their candidate.

Rabbi Raphael traveled to Berlin to the home of the great man. As he entered Mendelsohn's study, Rabbi Raphael was apprehensive, not knowing what to expect from a leader of Reform. He was reassured to see before him a serious-looking man seated at his desk, poring over an open volume of the Talmud.

Mendelsohn rose from his chair to greet the guest. Rabbi Raphael was shocked to see that his host's head was uncovered!

"A Jewish leader studies the Talmud without a hat!" thought Rabbi Raphael indignantly. "He studies Jewish law but does not observe its customs? And this is the man who must recommend me before I can become Chief Rabbi of Hamburg?"

"Shalom – Peace," said Mendelsohn, extending his hand in greeting to Rabbi Raphael.

"Peace?" answered Rabbi Raphael in anger. "There is no peace for the wicked! Are the people of Hamburg trying to mock me? Why do they send me to a heretical Jew for a recommendation? Better that I should become a beggar than that I should accept a recommendation from you!" And with that, Rabbi Raphael stalked out.

Mendelsohn lowered the hand he had extended in greeting and sat down to write his recommendation.

Burning with anger, Rabbi Raphael traveled back to Hamburg and went to the Jewish council. Ready to vent his outrage, Rabbi Raphael was pre-empted by the council leader.

"Welcome back, Rabbi! I wish to read to you the letter sent to us by Moses Mendelsohn." Before Rabbi Raphael could interject, the leader began reading.

"Greetings to my brethren in Hamburg. This is to report my impressions of the Rabbi you sent to me. He appears to be an honest and upright man with strong character. I find him to be a man of principles, committed to Jewish values. He will not be influenced to stray from what he believes is right. I therefore conclude that he is very well suited to be your Rabbi."

And so Rabbi Raphael became the Chief Rabbi of Hamburg.

An Insult May Be Strength Of Character In Disguise

Moses Mendelsohn has every right to be offended by the improper behavior of Rabbi Raphael, but he overcomes his justifiable outrage and looks beyond the immediate circumstances. His guest's rude reaction indicates certain personality traits that, under other circumstances, could be true assets.

A manager faces a similar task in assessing employees. It is easy enough to identify where an employee has succeeded or failed in his current surroundings. It is far more challenging and rewarding to analyze the personality traits that underlie the failures and place the employee in surroundings where his strengths can be best utilized and his weaknesses become irrelevant.

We might wonder how Rabbi Raphael felt about owing his job to the recommendation of a Reformer. Did it haunt him for the rest of his days and poison his attitude towards the people of Hamburg who had placed their faith in a heretic? Or, did Rabbi Raphael come to respect Mendelsohn's unflinching commitment to the public welfare, despite the personal affront he had endured?

We can hope that Rabbi Raphael came to realize that he had much to learn, even from a heretic, about leadership and maturity.

In Today's World

The story of the invention of masking tape illustrates the potential payoff in tolerating employee insubordination.

In the 1920's, 3M Corporation manufactured and sold abrasives. One afternoon, Dick Drew, a 3M inventor, visited an auto body shop in St. Paul, Minnesota to test a new batch of sandpaper. He overheard a group of workers cursing as they touched up the paint on a two-tone car. The workers explained that, before painting on the second color, they had to mask certain parts of the auto body, using a combination of heavy adhesive tape and butcher paper. Removing the tape often peeled away part of the new paint as well. The workers then had to go back and painstakingly touch up the flawed paint, resulting in extra labor, extra cost, and shoddy results.

Drew realized that what the customer needed was a tape that was less adhesive. He went back to the lab to search for the right combination of ingredients to create masking tape. After several months, 3M's President William L. McKnight ordered him to drop the project and get back to sandpaper. Drew ignored the directive. During one experiment, McKnight entered the lab, saw what Drew was working on, and silently continued walking.

Drew finally hit upon the right combination of materials and asked McKnight to approve funding to build a tape-making machine. McKnight refused, but Drew was undeterred. As a researcher, he had the right to approve purchases of up to $100, so he issued a flurry of $99 purchase orders for the needed parts. Once the machine was built, Drew showed it to McKnight and confessed his purchasing strategy.

History does not record McKnight's reaction, but we know that not only did Drew continue to work at 3M – masking tape quickly became their best-selling product.

McKnight could have fired Drew for insubordination. Instead, he defined 3M's management philosophy: "If you have the right person on the right project, and they are absolutely dedicated to finding a solution – leave them alone. Tolerate their initiative and trust them."[52]

Just remember – it takes the right person on the right project. Sometimes it is not a trivial feat to achieve this state of serendipity. Omit one of these ingredients, and you may find yourself quaffing a noxious brew of insubordination *and* failure.

A software company I worked for once hired an engineer named Bob Fabbio to develop a relational database. Bob completed his initial task within the first year, and then it quickly became apparent that Bob did not have a real interest in coding anymore. Given his ambitions to be much more than a software developer, he had lots of opinions about what the company was doing wrong, what products we ought to be developing, and what markets we should be pursuing. After a colorful year in which Bob clashed with many in R&D, he left the company and eventually moved to Austin. There he founded Tivoli, a software company that he ultimately sold to IBM for $745 million, far more than the market value of the company he had left.

There are two sides to the coin of personality. The same independence and determination that made it difficult for Bob to work as a software developer and accept the company's assumptions and choices made him a successful entrepreneur. Bob had to move on to another locale to reach his potential.

Perhaps it was no accident that Moses Mendelsohn, residing in Berlin, was able to overlook Rabbi Raphael's abrasiveness and recommend him as the Chief Rabbi of Hamburg, where he was far removed from Mendelsohn's day-to-day life. Even the tolerant Mendelsohn might have offered a different opinion had Rabbi Raphael applied for the same position in Berlin.

Lesson 24: Leave Room For Reward Regardless Of Results

Those Who Are Not Justified

In the days of Rabbi Dov Baer, the Great Preacher of Mezritch, a lad from Vitebsk named Anshel married a girl from a staunch anti-Hasidic family. Her father, who was well-to-do and influential, thoroughly investigated the prospective groom's family tree to insure that it harbored no trace of Hasidic leanings. Just to be sure, the cautious father stipulated that the financial support he would provide to the couple as Anshel continued his Talmudic studies was conditional upon the groom's remaining outside the Hasidic camp.

One day, Anshel came upon a passage in the Talmud that he could not fathom. No one in town could explain the passage to his satisfaction. Finally, in desperation, he went to the Hasidic synagogue at the edge of town, hoping that he might find there a book of commentary that would clarify the passage.

At the synagogue he met an elderly Hasid who asked him gently, "What is bothering you?" The young man laid out the puzzle, and the Hasid, without a moment of hesitation, explained the perplexing passage with clarity and sweetness.

Anshel began sneaking off to the Hasidic synagogue at every opportunity to study and to pray. Soon, wracked by his desire to learn more about Hasidism, Anshel ran away to Mezritch to study at the feet of the Great Preacher, Rabbi Dov Baer.

Anshel's father-in-law himself went to Mezritch to bring Anshel to his senses.

"If I had known you would become a Hasid, I would never have allowed you to marry my daughter," he railed. "The Hasidim have aberrant ways, and they violate Jewish law. You must return with me to Vitebsk, and swear that you will never rejoin the Hasidim. Otherwise, I will have your marriage to my daughter annulled, and you will be alone and penniless."

Torn but aware of his obligation, Anshel pledged to his father-in-law that he would come back to Vitebsk for good.

Once at home, Anshel was haunted by the pearls of Hasidic wisdom he had gleaned from the Great Preacher in Mezritch.

"Wisdom is there, and I am here," he thought to himself. "Without wisdom, I am no better than the animals of the field." After several months of agony, Anshel returned to Mezritch to learn Hasidism from the Great Preacher.

The father-in-law had seen enough. He asked the rabbi of Vitebsk to divorce the young couple on the grounds that Anshel had broken his solemn promise. The rabbi consulted the Code of Jewish Law and determined that a broken promise was indeed valid grounds for divorce. The rabbi granted the divorce, and Anshel thereby lost his livelihood. He lived in poverty for a few more years, fell ill and died.

Rabbi Dov Baer came to Vitebsk to eulogize Anshel. "Good people," he began, "we believe that when the Messiah comes, he will sit in judgment over all mankind. In this case, the father-in-law will claim innocence, as he consulted with the rabbi for a legal ruling. The rabbi will quote the relevant passage from the Code of Jewish Law to defend his ruling. Then the Messiah will ask Anshel, 'Why did you break your promise?' and Anshel will respond, 'I cannot justify my actions. I was wrong to break my promise. I simply had to go to learn from the Great Preacher.'"

"In the end, the Messiah will pronounce judgment. To the father-in-law he will say, 'You are acquitted, for you followed the rabbi's ruling.' To the rabbi he will say, 'You are acquitted, for you followed the Code of Jewish Law. But,' he will say, 'to acquit those who are justified, there is no need for the Messiah to sit in judgment. I have come to acquit those who are not justified. Anshel, you too are exonerated.'"

A Great Leader Can Reward Those Who Break The Rules

There is an inevitable tension between the letter of the law and the spirit of the law, between what is proper behavior in general and what is the correct action for a specific situation. One who follows the letter of the law will always find support for his actions. The Messiah in Rabbi Dov Baer's story comes to counterbalance the letter of the law, and provide support and comfort for those who follow the spirit of the law. They too have a champion who can appreciate their actions.

A manager uses many criteria to evaluate an employee's performance. Some managers reward people who accept the company line and follow procedures, others appreciate hard work, some emphasize pragmatism and the ability to deliver the product. It's easy enough to utilize these universally esteemed yardsticks. Over time, employees develop habits and responses and are typically rewarded for predictable and consistent performance.

Take a lesson from Rabbi Dov Baer and leave room in your management style to champion and appreciate less popular and harder-to-measure attributes like initiative and daring. Reward boldness, regardless of the eventual outcome, and you will build an aggressive and opportunistic organization; punish it, and you will create an army of mediocre yes-men.

In Today's World

There are times when operating by the book can, in fact, become a liability. Consider the case of Edward J. Smith, the captain of the Titanic, who, even after receiving an iceberg warning, continued full steam ahead. All his experience told him that anything big enough to sink a ship would be seen in time to maneuver around it.

But Smith had never captained a ship as large or as fast as the Titanic. As Brock Lovett says in the movie *Titanic,* he had "26 years of experience working against him.... Everything he knows is wrong."

When circumstances change, perhaps the most valuable action a person can perform is to question the rules.

The recent Columbia space shuttle disaster provides a striking example of when it pays to break the rules and how bureaucracy can work against an organization.

According to the independent Columbia Accident Investigation Board's report, eighty-two seconds after the shuttle lifted off on January 16, 2002, a 1.67-pound piece of foam struck the shuttle's left wing, opening a hole six inches wide. On January 17, a group of engineers watching a film of the launch at Marshall Space Flight Center noticed the foam strike.

To allow investigation of any possible damage, they made a highly unusual request to Linda Ham, chairwoman of the shuttle's mission management team at Johnson Space Center, that the Columbia maneuver itself into a position where its left wing could be photographed by a spy satellite. This would enable engineers to assess the damage, though it would also delay the mission and could delay future shuttle launches as well.

Separately, a group of low-level engineers led by Rodney Rocha was pursuing its own investigation, and decided there was no time for normal communication channels. Breaking all the rules, they turned directly to Ham on January 22 with an urgent request for photographs.

Ham received a third request for photographs from yet another team of engineers that same day.

According to the Investigation Board's report, Ham evidently rejected all three requests because none was made through the proper channels. Investigators concluded that Ham and the other leaders of the shuttle program had their priorities wrong – meeting the ambitious launch schedule was more important to them than safety.

Unfortunately for Columbia's crew, the engineers' understanding of when to break the rules was neutralized by bureaucratic procedures and processes, with tragic results.[53]

Chapter Summary: Lessons in Measuring Performance from the Hasidic Masters

Here is a recap of the lessons from the stories in this chapter.

Monitoring Schedules

- On-time delivery is not the be-all and end-all, but, *if you're going to be late, you'd better serve up a delicacy.*

Measurement and Management

- Measurement is not a substitute for management. *Don't just measure – nurture.*

Evaluating Performance

- Look beyond friction for personality traits that, under different circumstances, could be true assets. *An insult may be strength of character in disguise.*
- Leave room in your management style to champion and appreciate attributes, such as initiative and daring, which are unpopular and difficult to measure. *A great leader can reward those who break the rules.*

CHAPTER 5

Developing People

Dilbert, June 20, 2002

An opponent of Hasidism once said to Rabbi Yehuda Zvi of Rozdol, "It seems to me that to be a Rebbe is the greatest of all vices."

Rabbi Yehuda nodded his head in agreement. "You are right," he said to the man, "but to attain it, you must first master all the lesser vices."

"… a manager *develops people*. Through the way he manages he makes it easy or difficult for them to develop themselves. He directs people or misdirects them. He brings out what is in them or he stifles them. He strengthens their integrity or he corrupts them. He trains them to stand upright and strong or he deforms them… The manager is also responsible for developing himself."[54]

- Peter F. Drucker

א

A disciple chooses to follow the Rebbe who he believes can best advance his personal and spiritual development. The Rebbe, for his part, seeks to impart his core values to his followers, help them overcome and grow from their mistakes, and lead them to view a turbulent world from the proper perspective.

Even a Rebbe, like any manager, needs his own mentor – someone who can help him bear the burden and the privilege of leadership and guide him towards the proper balance in his own life between his power as a leader and his limitations as a human being.

Let's observe how the Hasidic Masters develop themselves and their teams: instilling core values, learning to cope with failure, and appreciating the burdens and rewards of leadership.

CORE VALUES

Lesson 25: The Team Reflects Your Core Values

The Preacher's Essence

Rabbi Meir of Premishlan received vast sums of money in gifts from his followers, who hoped their contributions would bring blessing upon themselves and their families. Rabbi Meir distributed all this money to the poor.

Once an itinerant preacher came to Premishlan. He was a learned man who traveled from town to town, delivering sermons in return for donations. The preacher delivered a well-received sermon in the town synagogue. But afterwards, when the caretaker took up a collection, the preacher was disappointed that the townspeople had donated only a few pennies.

Before leaving Premishlan, the preacher visited Rabbi Meir to receive his blessing and to ask for a donation. Rabbi Meir received the man graciously, sat with him for a few moments to discuss Jewish law, and gave him all the money that was in his pockets. Meanwhile, Hasidim continually streamed in, each with his request and his gift. Soon Rabbi Meir's table was covered with gold coins.

The preacher was jealous, and said to Rabbi Meir, "Rabbi, there is something I do not understand. You give short sermons on Hasidism, while I give long

152

discourses on the Torah. Why is it that people donate money so generously to you while they are so miserly with me?"

"The answer is simple," said Rabbi Meir. "Our audiences hear our words, but what they imitate are our inner attributes. They know that I despise money, and whenever I have a penny in my pocket I give it to a worthy cause. All who come to hear me are affected by my values – their money becomes worthless to them, so they leave it on my table. You, on the other hand – your entire goal in preaching is to receive money. You preach money, you desire money, you love money. When you preach, you transmit your own values to the people. Their money becomes very dear to them, and they are reluctant to give you more than a few precious pennies from their pockets."

Your Audience Hears Your Words, But They Imitate Your Values And Actions

The preacher's sermon may be learned and enlightening. Still, his audience sees through the ostensible message to the speaker's real values.

The same is true in the corporate world. If you preach cooperation, but your team is mired in backstabbing, consider whether the team is acting on their perception of what really matters to management. Their instinct, and the company's reward structure, may tell them that management pays mere lip service to the importance of cooperation. Re-examine core values – yours and the company's – and look at how words and actions may subliminally convey these values to the team.

In Today's World

One of the stiffest penalties ever imposed by the Securities and Exchange Commission was levied in 1991 on John Gutfreund, the CEO of Salomon, Inc. In addition to a $100,000 fine and revocation of his stock options and retirement benefits, Gutfreund was banned for life from serving as CEO of a securities firm.

Gutfreund merited this unprecedented punishment because he failed to censure one of his bond traders, Paul Mozer, when Mozer made illegal bids in auctions of Treasury notes in early 1991. By doing so, Gutfreund sent a clear message to his employees that it was acceptable to skirt the law so long as you were not caught.

Mozer violated federal law a second time in April of that year by buying nearly all the T-bills offered by the government in an open bid. Gutfreund knew about the violation but did not inform the government for several months. By the time he did so, the SEC had begun investigations, the story broke in *The Wall Street Journal*, and Salomon faced collapse as investors rushed to sell their Salomon debt securities.

Gutfreund resigned as CEO on August 18 of that year and appointed Warren Buffet as his replacement. Buffet relentlessly exposed Salomon's transgressions to the federal government and promoted Deryck Maugham, known as "Mister Integrity," to lead Salomon Brothers. By doing so, he sent a clear message to the employees of Salomon that he valued honesty and integrity above all else.[55]

In 1999, I opened a sales branch for News Digital Systems, a division of Rupert Murdoch's News Corporation, in office space in the News Corporation building in mid-town Manhattan.

Frank, the building manager, gave me an invaluable tip. "Whatever you do, don't put fresh flowers in the lobby."

"Why is that?" I asked.

"The office manager at another company brought in fresh flowers every day," Frank said. "One morning, Rupert came to visit and saw the flowers. He almost burst a blood vessel over the wastefulness, and fired the office manager on the spot."

I thanked Frank for the advice and ordered artificial shrubs. Murdoch had clearly succeeded in transmitting a core value of his company: thrift.

א

On a business trip to a Hewlett Packard plant in Colorado, I observed first-hand why HP maintains their reputation for high quality. Over lunch in the company cafeteria, I asked my host to tell me about HP. He regaled me with a story about the company's early days, when a calculator salesman would visit universities and attract buyers by slamming the rugged calculator against a wall, then nonchalantly demonstrate that it still crunched numbers accurately.

Another employee volunteered a story of a fire that had wiped out an entire computer center. At the bottom of the rubble, the firemen found an HP disk drive that still worked, its data intact.

Others eating around us chimed in with their own corporate legends. It was crystal clear that quality was a deeply ingrained value at HP.

Lesson 26: Do You Work To Live Or Live To Work?

Man and Mosquito

Once there was a Hasid named Zundel who earned his living by buying and selling horses. He worked hard and enjoyed his trade, but still found time every year to visit the court of his Master, Rabbi Isaac of Vorka.

On one such visit, Rabbi Isaac saw Zundel deep in animated conversation. Rabbi Isaac was pleased to see his followers discussing his teachings with such enthusiasm. Coming closer, Rabbi Isaac was disappointed to find that they were not discussing spiritual matters after all – Zundel was telling a story about a champion stallion! Several days later, Rabbi Isaac again overheard Zundel talking excitedly about a nag he had recently sold for a great profit.

A week passed. It was time for Zundel to return home, and he went to Rabbi Isaac to receive the customary blessing for the journey. Rabbi Isaac clasped Zundel's hand.

"Before I bless you, Zundel, please tell me, is there any question you have for me?"

Zundel was overjoyed at the opportunity to seek his master's advice. He launched into a description of a potential business deal involving a herd of mares. "Rebbe, please tell me," he concluded, "do you recommend I buy the herd or not?"

"May God grant you success in whatever path you choose," responded Rabbi Isaac, "so that you may continue to provide a good living for your horses."

Zundel was puzzled by his teacher's advice.

Rabbi Isaac continued, "Our sages once asked: why did God create man last among all the creatures during the six days of creation? They explained that the response is different for each and every man, depending on his behavior. If a man does good deeds and is worthy before God, we say, 'you were created last so that all God's creatures could be present to serve you.' If, on the other hand, a man is unworthy, we say, 'you were created last to teach you your true place in nature. Even the mosquito preceded you in creation and is more important in God's eyes.'"

Rabbi Isaac continued. "A man, by his thoughts and behavior, can raise himself so high that all of creation serves him, or he can lower himself to the point where his entire purpose in life is to feed mosquitoes with his blood! So, too, a horse trader can be worthy or unworthy. If he is worthy, God sends him horses so that he may support himself. If, on the other hand, he is unworthy, then God helps the horses He created by sending them a horse trader to support them. Both men earn the same living, but there is a world of difference between them. The worthy man has horses who work for him, while the unworthy man works all his life for his horses."

Zundel winced. Rabbi Isaac said kindly, "My blessing for you, Zundel, is that you merit to clean out your stable." Seeing Zundel's hurt look, Rabbi Isaac continued, "By spending all your waking hours thinking about your horses, I fear that you have turned your head into a stable, a place where only horses dwell. May you merit to clean out the stable, and find room in your mind for loftier thoughts."

Chastened but wiser, Zundel returned to his home.

The Worthy Man Works For His Living, While The Unworthy Man Lives For His Work

Nowadays we would call Zundel a workaholic. Even when he gets away to visit his Rebbe, he is still preoccupied with his business deals. Rabbi Isaac tries to show Zundel that his life is unbalanced – rather than utilizing his work as a means to spiritual growth, Zundel has become a slave to his horses. Only by "cleaning out his stable" can Zundel fulfill his potential as a human being.

Rabbi Isaac's advice is as sound today as it was then. A manager's work can be totally absorbing, to the point where it crowds out all other aspects of a well-balanced life. Ask yourself: do you work in order to live, or is work your life? Are you pouring all your energy into work, or is work one of many activities that enrich your life? And the same for the employees you manage – do you expect them to make work their life, or do you encourage them to keep work in its proper perspective?

To Rabbi Isaac, the answer to these questions determines whether you are the master or the slave of your environment.

In Today's World

SAS Institute, the provider of statistical analysis software for large databases, is an example of a company that does not compel its employees to choose between their work and their lives. The company's philosophy is simple: "The best way to produce the best and get the best results is to behave as if the people who are creating those things for you are important to you.... It just means you take care of the folks who are taking care of you."

Although SAS is in a highly competitive market, the company is famous for its thirty-five-hour workweek and generous family-oriented benefits. SAS provides on-site daycare and encourages employees to visit and eat lunch with their children during the day, coach their sports teams and be involved in their education. The spacious campus hosts weekend picnics and features a first-rate athletic facility, open to employees and their families.

It is tempting to think of SAS as a non-profit hippy commune, but nothing could be further from the truth. Their business analysis software must meet the exacting standards of large enterprises that require stable and predictable vendors. SAS software is used by more than 80% of the Fortune 500 companies, making SAS the largest private software company in the world, with annual sales of over $1.1 billion.

SAS stands out in its ability to build a successful business that is in harmony with, rather than in opposition to, their employees' family lives. SAS recognizes that employees have relationships outside of work, and provides benefits that help them effectively meet their family commitments. The results are impressive – more than twenty-four consecutive years of double-digit growth, a turnover rate of under 5%, and a workplace that attracts more than thirty applicants for each vacant position.[56]

Marc Benioff, the CEO of Salesforce.com, has fashioned an atmosphere that balances Silicon Valley's relentless drive with an eclectic blend of Eastern spirituality, parties and philanthropy.

After thirteen years at Oracle, frustrated by his inability to move his Internet-related activities into the company's spotlight, Benioff took a three-year leave of absence. He lived in Hawaii where he swam with the dolphins. Then he traveled to India, seeking enlightenment and career direction. One of the gurus he met there urged him to give back to the world even as he pursued his ambition.

Taking this advice to heart, Benioff returned to Oracle. Seeking to combine spirituality with technology, he helped Oracle CEO Larry Ellison set up a charitable foundation. But he wanted to go a step farther.

In the winter of 1999, Benioff left Oracle to start Salesforce.com, which sells software services delivered over the Internet to large enterprises. Rather than paying an up-front installation fee, corporations pay a monthly fee for each user, and don't have the headache of installing and maintaining software themselves. The upstart is gaining customers fast, and is threatening giants such as Siebel Systems, Oracle and PeopleSoft with its disruptive business model.

From the outset, Benioff decided that his company would engage in what he calls "compassionate capitalism." 1% of the company's stock, its profits and its employees' time go to charity. Benioff frequently shows up at work in a Hawaiian shirt with his golden retriever at his side, takes his managers swimming with the dolphins near his second home in Hawaii, and meditates to stay calm. The Dalai Lama was the keynote speaker at the company's celebration when it reached the 100,000-user mark.

Benioff believes that mixing personal interests with the best of traditional business practices creates an "integrated" company where people escape the traps of conventional thinking and work more creatively. "We need a constant reinforcement that we're a different sort of company with a different set of values," he says.[57]

When I was starting my career as a young engineer, I had an opportunity to observe the importance of maintaining a balanced life. There were two dominant technical managers where I worked: Rob, the Vice President of Research and Development, and Saul, the Chief Architect. Their personal styles were diametrically opposed.

Rob was a workaholic par excellence. Twice divorced, he had long ago decided that work was his life. He poured every drop of his energy into the company. He was the first to arrive in the morning and the last to leave at night. He never took a day's vacation and never talked about anything but work. Rob demanded the same total devotion from the development team that he did from himself.

Saul's approach was entirely different. He was a devoted husband and father and a rabid windsurfer. He was also an avid mountain climber, and would return from his death-defying expeditions with tales of danger and near-disaster. Besides all these extracurricular activities, Saul was also in charge of defining the functionality of the company's breakthrough product.

When I first joined this company as a programmer, Rob was the dominant figure in R&D. His drive and devotion spurred the engineers on to remarkable achievements. Saul, though recognized as a technical expert, left center stage to Rob.

As we commenced our second year of development, it was obvious to the engineers that Rob was burning out. His temper grew shorter, he reverted to a cigarette habit he had kicked years before, and the bags under his eyes sagged lower with each passing day. We saw the job draining the life out of Rob, like a mosquito draining its host of blood. He had no life outside of work, so he had nowhere to recharge his batteries.

Meanwhile, Saul was as energetic as ever. Each time he returned refreshed from a long weekend on the shore or an extreme mountaineering trek, we knew he would come back with some fantastic new idea for a product design improvement. The engineers began to gravitate towards Saul for technical advice and insight.

One morning, we arrived at work to discover that Rob was no longer in charge of R&D. The official explanation was that he was taking a leave of absence. Saul was appointed in his place, and R&D moved on without Rob.

For me, a young engineer, this was an eye-opening lesson. I had started out with the assumption that Rob's "pedal to the metal" style was an asset. Over time, I saw the work diminish Rob, to the point where he was no longer much use to himself or, ultimately, to the company. Saul, on the other hand, only gained strength as time went on. His work enriched his life, and his balanced interests outside of work ultimately enriched the company as well.

Lesson 27: Don't Trade Embarrassment For Shame

The Cabbage Hat

The followers of Rabbi Menachem Mendel of Kotsk were known for their extreme poverty and devotion to the truth. One of his Hasidim, Rabbi Shlomo, was so poor that he could not afford to buy a hat. He would keep his head dry with a cabbage leaf when he walked in the rain.

His father-in-law saw this public display of poverty.

"Aren't you ashamed to be seen wearing a cabbage leaf for a hat?" he asked Rabbi Shlomo.

Rabbi Shlomo was puzzled. "Why should I be ashamed? I didn't steal the cabbage leaf!"

> *There's No Shame In Wearing A Cabbage Leaf For A Hat, So Long As You Came By It Honestly*

Rabbi Shlomo's father-in-law has confused embarrassment with shame. Perhaps Rabbi Shlomo might be *embarrassed* by his poverty, and feel chagrin when he sees other families with more financial stability. But Rabbi Shlomo has no cause for shame – after all, he has done nothing dishonest which might bring him disgrace.

In business, a manager who achieves financial success, advancement or fame can feel justifiably proud. By contrast, managing an unsuccessful enterprise can be embarrassing.

But remember that there is no shame in failure if you gave the attempt your best try. Resist the seductive temptation to achieve success via dishonest means. You will find yourself simultaneously proud and ashamed, fearful of the disgrace that will come when your dishonesty is discovered – and, as the past few years' business headlines demonstrate, a great deal of dishonesty is eventually discovered.

In Today's World

Enron's executives were masters at converting embarrassment into shame. The energy giant ran up billions of dollars in debt, certainly an embarrassing performance. Rather than face an unpleasant reality, they embarked on a shameful campaign of deception, overstating income and hiding the astronomical debt from shareholders and employees via a labyrinth of phony partnerships, shell companies and fabricated subsidiaries.

In the short term, they avoided embarrassment, as they bolstered the price of their stock and continued to attract new investors. In the long term, they brought shame and ruin upon themselves, destroyed the jobs and retirement savings of their 11,000 employees, and toppled America's seventh largest company.

Enron's auditor, Arthur Andersen LLP, fared no better in resisting the temptation to convert embarrassment into wealth via subterfuge.

Enron paid their accounting firm $52 million per year for both accounting services and consulting services. As accountants, Andersen had an ethical obligation to objectively examine the company's balance sheets. But as well-paid consultants, they had a vested interest in their client's appearance of success. Andersen officials became committed accomplices to Enron's fraudulent practices.

As the scandal emerged, Andersen's lawyers instructed their employees to shred thousands of pages of documents that would have shed light on Enron's crimes. This attempt to cover up shameful behavior via even more shameful behavior backfired. Andersen was found guilty of obstructing justice, their customers fled to more reputable accounting firms, and the venerable accounting firm closed its doors in 2002.

א

Enabling computers to understand human speech is a challenging problem, as anyone who has used speech recognition software can attest. There are many technical difficulties: people talk at different speeds; accents differ; it is difficult to screen out background noise; choosing between homonyms requires not only voice processing but also semantic awareness.

The market leader in this area for many years was Lernout & Hauspie Speech Products NV (L&H), a publicly traded firm headquartered in Belgium. Unwilling to admit to flaws in their technology, L&H staged a number of fraudulent demonstrations. For example, at one Comdex show, co-founder Pol Hauspie led journalists through a breathtaking demonstration of a computer understanding human speech, until the software script that was simulating real voice recognition lost its place and got out of synch with the demonstrator's commands.

What drove L&H to falsify claims of the technology's capabilities? The company was under relentless pressure from investors to grow revenues and deliver results every quarter. This pressure also led L&H into a pattern of deceptive accounting practices designed to overstate sales.

A lot of creative accounting went into the doctoring of L&H's financial results. Many of the company's so-called customers were in fact "related parties," companies with whom L&H had investment ties. L&H routinely reported revenue from barter deals with other software companies in which no cash exchanged hands – the companies exchanged useless inventory, and both companies declared revenues. L&H even found a way to transform their internal research and development costs into revenue: they outsourced their own software development to wholly-owned subsidiary companies, then "bought" the resulting software. They declared revenues of $143.2 million for

1999 in far-off Singapore and Korea, where it was difficult for auditors to verify claims.

Co-founder Jo Lernout knew these were risky practices, but, as he was fond of saying, "The grass is always greener on the edge of the precipice." Buoyed by shady deals, L&H's revenues soared to $211.6 million in 1999, even though there remained a long way to go in developing both the technology and the market.

You can't fool all the people all the time, and you can't perpetually defer embarrassment by ever more shameful cover-ups. With their Korean revenues, L&H took one step too close to the precipice. On August 8, 2000, *The Wall Street Journal* reported that many of L&H's alleged Korean customers had, in reality, done no business with the company. An SEC probe followed and the cover-up started to unravel. L&H filed for Chapter 11 bankruptcy protection on November 29, 2000.[58]

Lesson 28: In Business, Truth Is Not An Absolute Value

Water in the Milk

Rabbi Menachem Mendel of Kotsk was known for his unflinching devotion to truth, no matter how uncomfortable and inconvenient the consequences.

Once a man came to Rabbi Menachem to unburden his conscience.

"Rebbe, I am a sinner, and I cannot stop my sinning. You see, I sell milk to the people of Kotsk, and I barely earn enough to support my family. In order to make ends meet, I am compelled to mix water into the milk. I know that I am cheating my customers, but I have no choice."

"Every man has free will, and can choose truth or falseness," replied Rabbi Menachem.

"If I do not dilute my milk, I will not earn a living," sighed the milkman.

"Nonetheless," Rabbi Menachem told the milkman, "you may not continue to cheat your customers. Promise me that, from this day forward, you will sell only pure milk, with no water mixed into it."

"I will do my best," pledged the milkman, and departed.

A few days later, the man returned weeping to Rabbi Menachem.

"I did as you requested," he cried, "and I have lost all my customers! When I come to deliver milk, they lock their doors before me. They say that my milk used to be fine, but lately it tastes too thick and is no longer fit to drink. They have all started buying from the other milkmen of Kotsk, all of whom water down their milk. The people are accustomed to the taste of watered-down milk!"

Rabbi Menachem reflected, then sighed.

"If that is the case," he said to the milkman, "go back to your customers and tell them that, from now on, you will supply them with the same milk as before. I permit you to dilute your milk with water. There is no other way – falseness has triumphed over truth."

When People Expect Water In Their Milk, Give Them Water In Their Milk

Rabbi Menachem discovers that truth is not an absolute value. Diluting the milk may be a minor fraud, but it is one that customers have come to expect, to the extent that they find the true taste of undiluted milk to be unpleasant. In the face of these conventions and expectations, Rabbi Menachem is compelled to permit falseness.

You may wonder why Rabbi Menachem gives in so easily. Why not encourage the milkman to expose the dishonesty of his peers? Rabbi Menachem seems to realize that such a path would only lead to more falsehood: the denials of the other milkmen, perhaps an attempt to discredit the honest milkman. And the bottom line is that the people have expressly opted for the form of the milk they receive for the price they are paying.

Rabbi Menachem comes to see that the problem is not superficial or localized – it is only one example of an inherent tension between business and ethics. While we may strive for ethical perfection, the world requires us to make some compromises with reality, with human nature, with the relative weights of costs and benefits, with the shades of gray on the continuum that sometimes exists between clear "right" and "wrong."

As Mark Twain once observed, "The secret of success is honesty and fair dealing. If you can fake those, you've got it made."

In Today's World

The young Thomas Edison learned a lesson about how people value absolute truth when he attempted to sell his first invention, a vote counting machine. The inventor was confident that the market would welcome a device that could vastly reduce the uncertainty and bickering associated with the election process.

Imagine his surprise when the legislature vetoed the purchase. A political boss explained realpolitik to the disappointed Edison, "Nobody wants that machine here because then they wouldn't be able to get away with selling their votes."[59]

The relationship between business and ethics has always been complex and prone to paradox. In recent years, companies such as The Body Shop, Starbucks Coffee and Ben & Jerry's Ice Cream have tried to take the high road, promoting their values and adopting a well-meaning corporate code of ethics. In the short term, such pronouncements have made for great publicity. But these companies have had difficulty producing the desired outcomes, despite their best intentions.

Take Starbucks, the Seattle-based coffee retailer, as an example. It was embarrassed by grassroots protests in 1994 because it bought beans from export houses that pay Guatemalan workers about $2.50 per day, far below a daily living wage. In response, Starbucks adopted a Thoreau-like code of conduct in 1995, vowing to purchase coffee only from suppliers committed to treating employees with respect and dignity.

But given the political morass in impoverished coffee-producing countries, Starbucks has no practical ability to oversee conditions or punish violators. Today, as in 1994, Guatemalan workers still earn less than the legal minimum wage and live in horrific conditions. While Starbucks earns "Corporate Conscience" awards, it would still cost a Guatemalan worker five days' salary to afford a pound of Starbucks coffee.[60]

Ben & Jerry's Ice Cream provides another case in point. The company will go down in the annals of business history as the first to turn a profit while behaving like a non-profit organization. Founder and former CEO Ben Cohen calls this approach "Caring Capitalism."

One of their most popular crusades is "Save the Rainforest," promoted on pints of Rainforest Crunch ice cream. The label proudly declares, "Money from these nuts will help Brazilian forest peoples start a nut-shelling cooperative that they'll own and operate."

At first, the money did indeed go to the Xapuri cooperative farm. But as the popularity of Rainforest Crunch ice cream grew, the struggling cooperative collapsed under the volume of nut orders that poured in. Ben & Jerry's ended up buying more than 95% of the nuts from commercial suppliers, some of whom were infamous for their violent handling of Brazilian labor disputes.

Even for the "forest peoples" themselves the project was a mixed blessing. The project's stated purpose was to support the rainforest farm cooperative, but a large percentage of the members abandoned their farms entirely. With their newfound wealth the forest peoples moved to urban homes, where many of them have struggled to adapt to a modern Western lifestyle.[61]

I do not mean to suggest that Starbucks or Ben & Jerry's acted out of dishonest or unethical intent. On the contrary, their stories illustrate how in the business world, even given the best of intentions, managers will still need to wrestle with complex dilemmas and paradoxes.

Taking Rabbi Menachem's advice, perhaps these companies should stop proclaiming absolute virtue, and look instead for the smallest possible untruth that brings the largest possible good.

The first time I made a job offer to a potential employee, I brought my own straightforward style to the negotiations. Alan had exactly the talents we were seeking, and there were lots of companies looking for people with his skill set. My Human Resources Director suggested I offer Alan a mid-range salary and leave myself room to sweeten the offer, if that was needed to clinch the deal. But I was sure that honesty was the best policy, so I offered Alan the highest salary I could afford, telling him with all sincerity, "It's a great offer, with no beating around the bush. That's the kind of organization we run – no nonsense or posturing."

To my surprise, Alan called me back a few days later to ask whether we could increase our offer. I had left myself no leeway and could not offer him a penny more. Alan signed with a rival company for the same salary I had offered him. He told me that he concluded, from the fact that they had sweetened their originally low offer, that the other company was more determined to bring him on board.

COPING WITH FAILURE

Lesson 29: A Single Success Can Outweigh Many Failures

The Persistence of a Thief

Rabbi Moshe Leib of Sasov spared no effort to help ransom Jewish families from debtor's prison, where they would otherwise have been left to die for failing to repay their debts to the local Lord Mayor. Whenever the Jewish community required donations to pay such a debt, Rabbi Moshe would stop whatever he was doing and collect money from door to door. His prestige and persuasiveness helped save many a Jewish family from death.

Sometimes the community fell short of the needed sum. One especially hard year, the debts were so heavy that the community simply could not cover them. Rabbi Moshe's efforts to collect money to ransom families repeatedly fell short.

Returning home from yet another failed mission, he thought to himself, "God is not with me, otherwise I would be more successful. Perhaps God is angry with me for interrupting my study and prayer. I will stay home and let God send someone whom He will bless with success to do this rescue work."

Rabbi Moshe's thoughts were interrupted by the hysterical wailing of Freidel, the wife of Ezekiel the Thief.

"My Ezekiel – they're beating him to death!" she cried.

Ezekiel had been caught red-handed stealing alms from the church. The police had taken him to their barracks, where they were beating him without mercy.

Freidel ran to Rabbi Moshe. "Rabbi Moshe, you know my Ezekiel – he means no harm. The police respect you as a holy man, and will listen to you. Only you can save him. I beg you – please go to the police and plead for his life!"

Rabbi Moshe did indeed know Ezekiel the Thief. He had spent many hours trying without success to convince him to take up a different line of work. It was no use – Ezekiel genuinely loved his vocation.

It made no difference to Ezekiel whether the prize was a penny or a hundred gold coins – he thrilled to the challenge of pulling off a successful robbery. If Ezekiel left a room without stealing something, he felt that he had left behind something of his own. If a few days passed without an opportunity to steal, Ezekiel would practice on himself, sneaking into his own room and pocketing his own wallet. He defied any efforts to persuade him that theft was wrong.

"As much as I don't approve of Ezekiel's behavior," thought Rabbi Moshe, "his life is at stake."

"I will do my best, and may God help us," he said to Freidel, and hurried off to the police barracks.

There he saw Ezekiel, bloodied and beaten. The police chief respected the Jewish holy man, and listened to Rabbi Moshe's pleas for Ezekiel's life. He deliberated for only a few moments.

"Out of respect for you, I am willing to free him, but on one condition. You must take responsibility to ensure that he never steals again."

Rabbi Moshe accepted the offer with gratitude and escorted out the battered and bloody Ezekiel.

"Look at yourself, Ezekiel!" said Rabbi Moshe. "Your thievery has almost cost you your life. If you want to avoid this fate, you must swear to me that you will never steal again."

Ezekiel looked insulted. "Rabbi, just because I am a thief, do you think I am also a liar? I will not swear a false oath. Of course I will continue to steal!"

Rabbi Moshe was stunned. "The blood is still fresh from the beating you received for stealing. Do you understand the consequences of your actions?"

Ezekiel waved his hand dismissively. "This time I failed and I was caught. And even if next time I also fail – why, I may succeed the time after that. Don't you see, Rabbi Moshe? The failures do not matter – a single success more than repays the price of all the failures."

The words of Ezekiel the Thief left a deep impression on Rabbi Moshe.

"We are instructed to learn from every man," thought Rabbi Moshe. "I can learn much from Ezekiel's dedication to his calling. 'The failures do not matter – a single success more than repays the price of all the failures.'"

"How much more so is this true of my efforts to ransom debtors. Though my recent efforts have not met with success, the failures should not deter me. Perhaps my next mission will succeed. I must keep trying."

And Rabbi Moshe resumed his rescue activities as before.

A Single Success Can More Than Repay The Price Of Many Failures

Nowadays we might call Ezekiel a serial entrepreneur, repeatedly engaging in high-risk activities involving other people's money. His persistence and his resilience in the face of failure teach us an important lesson, one that applies to other endeavors besides thievery.

Every manager inevitably encounters failure. A recent UK survey determined that most information technology projects fail: the average time overrun is 222%, and over 31% of these projects are cancelled entirely. Yet we know that many projects do succeed, and that the field of information technology has taken great strides forward.

A more important question than whether you will fail is how you will respond to failure and what you will learn from it. Your initial response, like Rabbi Moshe's, may be the natural instinct to flee and try your hand at something with a higher chance of success. It takes experience and fortitude to reach Ezekiel's level of commitment to persist in the face of failure.

Failure in an organization can actually be a positive sign – it shows that employees are willing to take the risks required to succeed. Some attempts may fail, but, as hockey great Wayne Gretzky once said, "You miss 100% of the shots you don't take." Coca Cola's former CEO, Roberto Goizueta, put it this way: "If you take risks, you may fail. If you do not take risks, you will surely fail."

Exemplary leaders seek to create a climate that tolerates failure. The alternative – an environment where people take no risks and cover up their mistakes – is far more costly. William McKnight, president of 3M, made this principle a basis for 3M's organizational culture: "Mistakes will be made. But, if a person is essentially right, the mistakes he or she makes are not as serious in the long run as the mistake management will make if it undertakes to tell those in authority exactly how they must do their jobs. Management that is destructively critical when mistakes are made kills initiative. And it's essential that we have many people with initiative if we are to continue to grow."[62]

Rabbi Moshe needs to learn fortitude. Ezekiel needs to learn when fearlessness crosses the line to become foolishness. Now that the police have their eye on him, he must "know when to fold 'em," when to walk away from a high-risk enterprise while he is still ahead. You won't have a chance to apply what you learn from your failures unless you live to tell the tale.

In Today's World

Thomas Edison spent the winter of 1879 trying to perfect the light bulb. The problem was finding the right filament, one that would conduct light without giving off too much heat. Edison tested a variety of materials, including copper, steel, metal and various alloys. But none of the materials he tested worked. Edison failed over 10,000 times before he hit upon carbonized cardboard as the perfect filament for the light bulb.

When a reporter subsequently asked him how it felt to fail over 10,000 times, Edison responded, "I didn't fail. I just discovered 10,000 ways not to invent the light bulb."

Edison went on to receive 1,093 patents, more than any other person in U.S. history.

The first products of many established and venerable corporations flopped. Would you have guessed that Sony's first product, a rice cooker, didn't work properly and failed to sell? Minnesota Mining & Manufacturing, later 3M, began their corporate existence running a failed corundum mine. Hewlett-Packard racked up a number of initial product failures, including electronic bowling alley sensors, a shock machine for weight loss and an automatic urinal flusher, before it hit upon a winner —the audio oscilloscope.

These companies learned from their early failures and grew into top-flight organizations that consistently come up with outstanding products and excel at bringing them to market.[63]

Lesson 30: Look For The Right Path Together

Let Us Share Our Mistakes

During the period of reflection and repentance before the High Holy Days, Rabbi Haim of Tsanz would tell his Hasidim stories to inspire them to return to God. He once told the following tale:

"Once a man lost his way in the forest. He wandered for weeks, looking for a road that would lead him back to civilization. But every path he tried only took him deeper into the forest.

One day, another man who was lost in the forest chanced upon the first man. Overjoyed, he exclaimed, 'Thank goodness I have found you! Can you please show me the way out of the forest?'

The first man laughed sadly. 'You assume that I know the way out, but you are mistaken. I am as lost as you are.'

The second man's joy turned to panic. 'Then you are no help at all! What will become of us?'

The first man thought. 'I do believe I can help you,' he said. 'If you know the roads I have taken that only lead further into the forest, it will save you the trouble of trying those roads yourself. You can help me in the same way, by telling me all the trails you have tried. Then, we can look for the right path together.'"

"So it is with us, my Hasidim," concluded Rabbi Haim. "We are all lost, and each of us has tried the wrong path. Let us share our mistakes, and look for the right path together."

Share What You Know About The Wrong Path

Mistakes happen in business. When you, as a manager, make a mistake, you'll have to take responsibility for the consequences. When your team members make mistakes, you will need to help them to do the same.

At the same time, try to use mistakes to educate yourself and others. Make sure everyone in the team learns from the errors – yours, theirs, and other team members'. The technique of "post-mortem" project analysis helps the team to acknowledge, and consciously formulate what they have learned from their successes and missteps, and to compile this information in a form useful for shaping future decisions.

Try to ensure that all the mistakes in your organization are new mistakes, rather than repeat trips down paths that have already been proven wrong. At least the company will derive some profit from your errors.

In Today's World

An apocryphal IBM anecdote tells of a new employee who, having just made a million-dollar mistake, was called into his manager's office. He went with understandable apprehension.

"Are you going to fire me now?" he asked.

"How can I fire you?" replied his manager. "I just spent a million dollars on your education!"

Steve Case, the chairman of America On Line (AOL), led the historic merger between AOL and Time-Warner in 1999, but could not make it succeed, and ultimately was forced to resign in 2003. Among the factors leading to Case's downfall was his inability to acknowledge his mistakes and learn from them.

Even when it became clear that his strategy was not meeting shareholder expectations, Case continued to act as if the merger had been a success.

"He doesn't second-guess himself or have any regrets," said one executive at AOL Time Warner. Surely speaking for many of his colleagues, he continued, "I would feel a lot better about [the current situation] if Steve said he made a bunch of mistakes."[64]

Most Silicon Valley venture capitalists prefer to back people who've previously founded firms and failed rather than those who are new to the business. Rather than being a stigma, failure is treated as a badge of honor, "like a dueling scar in a Prussian officer's mess."[65]

For example, venture capitalist John Doerr financed entrepreneur Jerry Kaplan's company Go, a pen-computing start-up, in the early 1990's. Go burned through over $90 million of cash in two years, a spectacular failure even by Silicon Valley standards.

A few years later, when Kaplan had another idea for an online auction Web site, he went right back to Doerr for financing. You may find it hard to believe, but Doerr agreed.

Today Kaplan's new company, OnSale, is a resounding success, Kaplan is a multi-millionaire, and Doerr has turned a handsome profit.[66]

In his book *Geeks and Geezers: How Era, Values, and Defining Moments Shape Leaders*, Warren Bennis observed this phenomenon among respected business executives. Most had passed through a crucible – a traumatic experience that tested them to their cores, strengthened them, and empowered them personally to achieve success later in life.

In such situations, with everything at stake and the outcome uncertain, these future leaders found their "true north." Having survived the crucible, they emerged as stronger individuals, confident they could take on any challenge.

Those who avoid the crucible will find themselves less prepared for real-world challenges and will run a higher risk of making major mistakes.[67]

BEING A LEADER

Lesson 31: You're Not A Leader In Every Situation

In the Bathhouse

Rabbi Ayzel Kharif, the Chief Rabbi of the town of Slonim, was washing in the public bathhouse one Friday afternoon in preparation for the Sabbath. Standing naked in a pool of steaming water, he closed his eyes and relaxed.

One of the townspeople mistook him from behind for an old friend, and playfully splashed cold water on his back. Rabbi Ayzel turned around with a start, and the man almost fainted – instead of playing his prank on a friend, he had teased the Rabbi himself!

"Rebbe, please forgive me," stammered the man. "I did not know.... "

Rabbi Ayzel smiled at the man. "Do not worry. I am not upset. After all, I am not a Rebbe from behind."

A Leader Is Not A Leader From Every Angle

The New Rabbi's Test

When the time came for the Jews of Prague to select a chief rabbi, they offered the position to Rabbi Ezekiel Landau, the renowned Talmudic scholar from the town of Brodie. The decision was far from unanimous.

"After all," some said, "are there not Torah scholars born and raised in Prague who are also worthy of the office?"

Rabbi Ezekiel's opponents devised a plot to discredit him.

"When the new Rabbi arrives, the town will hold a festive meal in his honor. We will pay someone to bring the Rabbi a difficult case regarding the kosher status of a chicken, one that has room for either leniency or stringency. The scholars among us will study all possible facets of the case thoroughly in advance. The Rabbi, on the other hand, will be unprepared. We will refute whatever answer he gives, proving that the scholars of Prague are superior to the new Rabbi from Brodie."

The day Rabbi Ezekiel arrived, the Jews of Prague greeted him with a banquet. During the meal, as planned, a man brought his question to the new Rabbi. The man described how he had slaughtered his chicken and what signs he had found inside the chicken.

"So, Rabbi, please tell me, may I eat the chicken or not?" he asked.

Rabbi Landau listened carefully to the facts of the case and thought for several minutes. He expounded the legal aspects of the situation to the community leaders and concluded, "I see enough legal basis to declare this chicken kosher."

The scholars of Prague pounced. They proceeded to refute Rabbi Ezekiel's arguments one by one. The Rabbi defended his ruling, but his impromptu reasoning was no match for the well-prepared logic of his opponents.

Finally, Rabbi Ezekiel conceded with modesty, "My ruling was incorrect. The chicken is, in fact, unkosher, and may not be eaten."

The banquet hall fell silent as the community leaders looked at each other in amazement. Their new Rabbi had erred in his very first ruling, and the local scholars had had to correct him! Perhaps Rabbi Ezekiel was a poor choice for Chief Rabbi?

Rabbi Ezekiel broke the uncomfortable silence.

"Wise men of Prague, perhaps you can provide an answer for a question which has troubled me for many years. It is the custom in every Jewish community to appoint a single man to be the Chief Rabbi, and that one man, all by himself, decides all matters of Jewish law. Is it not remarkable that an entire community should put its trust in one man's judgment? After all, the Chief Rabbi is only human, and is as likely to err as the next man. Why does the community not suspect their Rabbi's rulings?"

Rabbi Ezekiel waited for a response from the scholars and leaders of Prague. None of them spoke nor looked him in the eye.

Rabbi Ezekiel continued, "If you do not know, I will explain it to you. The community does their part by choosing a Chief Rabbi who is God-fearing, learned, and who takes the needs of the community seriously. The Rabbi does his part by carefully weighing the merits of each case that is brought to him before he issues a ruling. The Rabbi relies on his training, experience and instincts to arrive at what he hopes is the proper decision. If the community and the Rabbi have faithfully carried out their roles, then we believe that God will do His part, and reward them with the help they need to arrive at the correct ruling."

"But when does this apply?" asked Rabbi Ezekiel. "When the case that comes before the Rabbi is a real one, in which a real person awaits real guidance – then we believe that the Rabbi, with God's help, will arrive at the correct ruling. However, if the case is a fabrication – then there is no divine guidance at work. It is simply a matter of logic and preparation. In such cases, the Chief Rabbi's opinion is no better than anyone else's."

"In this case which has come before me now," he continued, "I see that my ruling can be refuted by the wise scholars of Prague. I must therefore conclude that this is not a real case, but one which has been contrived to test my skills."

Rabbi Ezekiel's opponents were so impressed by the wisdom of their new Chief Rabbi that they became his devoted followers.

In Matters Of Logic And Preparation, The Leader's Opinion Is No Better Than Anyone Else's

Rabbi Ayzel and Rabbi Ezekiel are both distinguished leaders who rely upon their expertise, their instincts and a little divine guidance to help them make the right decisions when steering their followers. But in their wisdom, they know the limits of their power, and recognize situations where their leadership is irrelevant. Naked in the bathhouse, or arguing a logical position, even the Chief Rabbi has no more rights or authority than any other man.

Your power as a manager comes with a similar disclaimer. Your organization gives you a high degree of control over decisions affecting your team – how much they will earn, what tasks they will perform and with whom, how their personal achievements will be measured. When faced with a problem within those boundaries, you rely upon your expertise and instincts to make the right call. Unlike Rabbi Ezekiel, most managers cannot claim divine guidance, although many could use it.

But beware: this power can be intoxicating, to the point where you forget the limits of your jurisdiction. In brainstorming sessions or technical discussions, resist the temptation to "pull rank" and impose your own opinion without really hearing the alternatives. Managers are generally chosen, or should be, for other qualities than their technical brilliance or recent hands-on expertise. Your team members may well be more qualified than you are to offer technical opinions, and more qualified opinions should carry more weight.

Likewise, managers should not abuse their positions of power to impose their own political opinions or religious beliefs on their teams in areas not related to the stated mission and values of the organization. Doing so undermines the manager's overall effectiveness in getting the real job done.

In Today's World

Management professor Henry Mintzberg points out that we keep upping the ante, moving beyond leaders who merely lead, to heroes who save.

The business press tends to portray corporate leaders as lone cowboys in either white or black hats, single-handedly responsible for the success or failure of their companies. John Scully at Apple, Lee Iacocca at Chrysler, Jack Welch at General Electric, Lou Gerstner at IBM – all have been alternately deified and vilified as their companies' fortunes rise and fall.

Mintzberg offers a quote from a *Fortune* article to support his point. "When Merck's directors tapped Raymond Gilmartin, 56, as CEO four years ago, they gave him a crucial mission: Create a new generation of blockbuster drugs to replace important products whose patents were soon to expire. Gilmartin has delivered."

Mintzberg reflects, "You would think he had his hands full managing the company. Yet there he apparently was, in the labs, developing those drugs. And in just four years at that. From scratch."

Another *Fortune* article proclaimed, "In four years, Gerstner has added more than $40 billion to IBM's share value."

Mintzberg muses, "Every penny of it! Nothing from the hundreds of thousands of other IBM employees. No role for the complex web of skills and relationships that people form. No contribution from luck. No help from a growing economy. Just Gerstner."

Mintzberg's conclusion is that the role of management is overrated. "The manager is not the organization, any more than a coat of paint is what holds up a building.... A healthy organization does not leap from one hero to another; it is a collective social system that naturally survives changes in leadership."

The best managers, according to Mintzberg, manage quietly, exercising thoughtfulness rooted in experience. They are not necessarily the personalities the press lauds as superheroes – in fact they may deliberately keep a very low profile.

"If you want to test the above proposition, try Switzerland," he suggests. "It is a well-run country. No turnarounds. Ask the next Swiss you meet the name of the head of state. Don't be surprised if he or she does not know. The seven people who run the country sit around a table, rotating that position on an annual basis."[68]

One morning, in my first week on a new job as Vice President of Research & Development, as I walked towards the company's only bathroom, I saw Fred, one of the junior programmers, heading for the same destination. When Fred spotted me, he stopped to let me pass. "No, thanks," I said, "Go ahead. You were first."

"No, you go first," protested Fred. "After all, you're a manager."

I refused, and Fred went into the bathroom. I had several moments to stand there waiting for Fred, as I contemplated my predecessor, the previous head of R&D, who had actually managed to convince his team that a manager's bladder was more important than theirs.

Lesson 32: Square Your Shoulders And Take The Blame

The Ninth Day of Passover

It was past midnight, and nearly all the Jews of Prague were asleep. Tomorrow was the eighth and last day of Passover. Leaving the synagogue at the end of the coming day, the Jews would be surrounded by the commotion of non-Jewish bakers selling bread. Since Jews are forbidden to eat or prepare leavened foods on Passover, the non-Jewish bakers of Prague were anticipating an annual business opportunity – to provide the Jews with fresh hot bread at the conclusion of Passover.

Even at this late hour, one Jew was still awake. Rabbi Ezekiel Landau, spiritual leader of the Jews of Prague, was laboring over the next day's sermon by the light of a flickering candle. He was interrupted by a soft knock at the door.

Surprised that anyone was still up and about, Rabbi Ezekiel opened the door. Before him stood a young Gentile peasant.

"I must speak with you. Please let me in!" whispered the boy.

"Don't you recognize me, Rabbi?" asked the boy once he was inside. "I am Pavel the orphan!"

Rabbi Ezekiel's face lit up. "Pavel, how you've grown! Years have passed since we last talked."

Pavel nodded. "I remember our talks with great fondness. You always invited me in for a bite to eat when I passed by your home late at night after a long day of labor."

"Tell me, Pavel, what have you been doing these past few years?" asked Rabbi Ezekiel.

"I am an apprentice to Nicholas the yeast brewer," replied Pavel.

Rabbi Ezekiel winced at the mention of Nicholas, known throughout Prague for his hatred of the Jews.

"That is why I have come to you this evening," said Pavel. "My master Nicholas is part of a conspiracy to kill the Jews of Prague! Tomorrow the bakers of Prague will buy yeast from Nicholas for the bread they will bake to sell to the Jews as they leave the synagogue tomorrow night. Nicholas intends to sell them poisoned yeast. All the bread outside the synagogue will be poisoned, and the Jews who eat it will die!"

Pavel continued, "I have come to tell you this because I remember your kindness to me. But you must not tell anyone that you know about this plot. Otherwise, Nicholas will deduce that I am the one who informed the Jews of the plot and he will kill me."

Rabbi Ezekiel listened carefully as he stroked his beard, deep in thought.

"Pavel, I thank you for your bravery in coming. You have more than repaid whatever kindness I showed you when you were a child. By coming here, you have entrusted me with your life, and I will not betray that trust. No one will ever know that I have been told about this plot. I will devise some way to save my people that will not give away the fact that I was warned. As for you, please hurry back to Nicholas' house before he notices you are missing."

Rabbi Ezekiel hugged Pavel and saw him out. He then returned to his desk, and began working on quite a different sermon.

The next morning, on the eighth and final day of Passover, the Altneu synagogue was filled to capacity. All the Jews of Prague came to pray and to hear Rabbi Ezekiel's sermon. When the time came, Rabbi Ezekiel faced the congregation from the pulpit.

"I have been studying the Jewish calendar for the past few days, and I have come to a conclusion which I must share with you. I, the Chief Rabbi of Prague, have erred in my calculation of the Jewish dates. Because of my error, we started observing the holiday of Passover one day too early. Today is not the eighth day of Passover – it is the seventh day! I accept full responsibility for this error, and I beg your forgiveness. I thank God that I discovered this error in time, before the end of Passover. I hereby declare that Passover does not end tonight – Passover will end tomorrow night!"

The congregants sat in stunned silence, then began whispering to each other. The Jewish community of Prague was abuzz. How could their great Rabbi, the leader of the generation, make such an egregious error? It seemed inconceivable. Businessmen who had suffered monetary loss from the Rabbi's legal rulings murmured, "Perhaps he has erred in other matters as well?"

But their Chief Rabbi had ruled, and the community accepted his ruling. At the conclusion of the service, Rabbi Ezekiel left the synagogue quickly.

That evening, after the holiday prayer, as the congregation exited the synagogue, they were surprised to see the non-Jewish bakers waiting outside, clamoring to sell hot bread to the Jews at the conclusion of Passover. The congregants apologized to them and explained the Rabbi's error.

When the bakers heard this, they threw their bread on the ground in disgust. "Why should we suffer just because your Rabbi made a mistake!" they shouted.

189

"What are we to do with the bread now? By morning it will be too stale to sell!"

A passing dog gobbled down a discarded roll and began to howl and foam at the mouth. Within moments, the dog lay dead.

A crowd gathered. Someone shouted, "The dog died from eating the bread!" The bakers fed a loaf to another dog, and soon that animal too was writhing on the ground in agony.

The bakers called the local authorities, who quickly determined that the yeast had been poisoned. They arrested Nicholas the yeast brewer, and the plot to poison the Jews was discovered.

As for the Jews of Prague, they kept an extra day of Passover that year, as their Rabbi had decreed. In later years, whenever they recalled this incident, they would say with reverence, "Our Rabbi is indeed the leader of the generation. He is so holy that even his mistakes bring blessing."

A Great Leader Takes Responsibility For Mistakes He Did Not Make

This story illustrates the burden of leadership. Rabbi Ezekiel possesses information he must keep to himself, to protect both his community and his source. For the good of his flock, he must inflict upon them an uncomfortable and inconvenient last-minute change. In order to save the community, he must publicly admit to an egregious error he did not commit, sacrificing his own prestige. Rabbi Ezekiel's decision is lonely and difficult, though by the end of the story, his wisdom is appreciated by all.

In the business world, the leader has to make similarly unpopular decisions, often without such a happy ending. You sometimes must take the blame for errors you did not commit, sacrificing your own prestige for the long-term good of the organization. As a manager, you must plan ahead based on information you cannot share, taking actions that seem unfathomable or worse to your team.

In trying to get people to work differently, you inevitably take them out of their comfort zone and awaken antagonism and resistance, a process Heifitz and Linsky refer to as "disappointing people at a rate they can absorb."[69] And you sometimes must take the blame for errors you did not commit, sacrificing your own prestige for the long-term good of the organization. As Max DePree, the former chief executive of furniture manufacturer Herman Miller, once commented, "Leaders don't inflict pain; they bear pain."[70]

These personal challenges – the stress of heavy responsibility, the occasional resentful responses of team members, behind-the-scenes political maneuvering – are part of the personal toll a management role can take on you. They are an unavoidable part of the job. If this seems to you to be too high a price to pay, consider looking for another line of work.

In Today's World

The United States launched a failed attempt to overthrow Cuba's Communist government in April of 1961 in an operation known as the Bay of Pigs.

The CIA had planned the botched operation, and, according to the agency's own internal inquiry, bore most of the blame for the fiasco. None of the CIA officers involved knew Spanish or had any understanding of Cuban internal politics; they treated the Cuban invasion force "like dirt" by providing them with inadequate training and weapons; and they failed to explain the details of the operation to newly inaugurated President John F. Kennedy.

Privately, Kennedy was convinced that he'd been deceived by the CIA, who had failed to inform him of the risks surrounding the invasion. But on the fourth day of the invasion, once it was obvious that the operation had failed, Kennedy, as President, publicly accepted full responsibility for the disaster. This act only added to his prestige, and enhanced his presidential image as a leader who willingly accepted the burdens of the office.

In parallel, Kennedy orchestrated damage control efforts. He sent his spin-doctors to make sure that influential columnists and TV reporters knew that the CIA was really to blame. JFK was quoted, off the record, as having said to his favored columnists, "How could I have been so stupid to trust such a gang?"[71]

Kennedy learned from his mistake and re-shaped his foreign policy decision-making structure so that he was not dependent on a narrow group of advisors. He learned to question others' assumptions and values, to critically examine the intelligence brought to him, and to reach down into the bureaucracy to obtain unfiltered information. This seasoned approach contributed to his success in handling the Cuban Missile Crisis in 1963.

Management consultant Barry Maher tells the following story:

"A corporation that had recently become a Wall Street darling had to announce that they'd miscalculated their earnings for the previous quarter. The stock price plummeted. The next day I was called in for a little damage control. The volatile chief financial officer was hardly the most popular person in the company, and I walked into his outer office just in time to catch his matronly secretary facing out the window with her sweater pulled up around her shoulders."

"At first I thought she was flashing her fellow workers as they arrived in the employee parking lot below. Then she turned toward me in surprise. Before she could pull the sweater back down, I caught a quick glimpse of the tee shirt she was wearing underneath. It read: 'Mistakes have been made. Others will be blamed.' A few minutes later, I discovered that she'd done an excellent job of anticipating her boss's strategy. As Fran Leibowitz said, 'It's not whether you win or lose, it's how you lay the blame.' But the chief financial officer's failure to accept the blame was the main reason he later lost his job."[72]

Lesson 33: You Are Fortunate To Be A Manager

You Are Indeed Fortunate...

Once a Hasid named Aharon had a daughter who reached marriageable age. Naturally, marriage was too serious a matter to be left in the hands of an immature young bride or groom. After a lengthy search, Aharon identified a suitable groom. The boy was a promising young Talmud scholar from a distinguished line of rabbis, and his father was a well-to-do businessman in a distant town. The parents met and finalized the arrangements. The young couple became engaged, and the wedding date was set for a year hence.

The months passed quickly, and Aharon's family began preparations for a gala wedding. Their exuberance was cut short one day when a letter arrived from the groom's father.

"This past year has been a difficult one for us," the letter began. "Disaster has befallen my business, and I have lost my fortune. I am now penniless, and am unable to honor my financial commitments to the bride and groom. I pray that your fortune has been better than mine, and look forward to dancing at our children's wedding."

Aharon was shocked and outraged – shocked at the thought that his daughter would marry a pauper, and outraged at the gall of the groom's father in assuming that the wedding should proceed despite his inability to hold up his end of the contract.

Aharon's first instinct was to take the letter to the town's Chief Rabbi and ask to have the marriage contract annulled. But on the way, he calmed down and re-considered. While Aharon was not a scholar, he knew enough about Jewish law to realize that this was far from an open-and-shut case. After all, the groom's parents had entered into the marriage agreement in good faith, and were unable to fulfill their obligations through no fault of their own. The legal ruling – to annul or carry out the wedding contract – would be a subjective decision as to the intent and expectations of each side.

"No," thought Aharon, "the local rabbi cannot be trusted to issue the correct ruling. Which rabbi should I turn to, which rabbi can I rely on to cancel the wedding?"

"I will turn to my Rebbe, Rabbi Shmelke of Nicholsburg," decided Aharon. "He has known me since I was a child, and he knows that I want only the best for my daughter. I will travel to Nicholsburg and ask Rabbi Shmelke to judge this case."

Arriving in Nicholsburg on a Friday afternoon, Aharon went directly to pay his respects to Rabbi Shmelke.

"What brings you here before the High Holidays?" Rabbi Shmelke asked Aharon, "Is everything well with you?"

"No, Rebbe. All is not well. I have a serious problem." And Aharon proceeded to spell out his predicament.

"Rebbe, I have come here to ask you to judge this case," concluded Aharon.

Rabbi Shmelke smiled at Aharon. "You are indeed fortunate that you have come to me for a ruling," he said. Aharon felt relief that the burden had been lifted from his shoulders.

"But now," continued Rabbi Shmelke, "the Holy Sabbath is almost upon us. Please erase all worry from your mind and enjoy the Sabbath at my table. On Sunday, I will convene the court and issue a ruling in your case."

Aharon was elated, and enjoyed the Sabbath as if it were a taste of the world to come. Besides the pleasures of a visit to his Rebbe's court, Aharon knew he had been wise to place his trust in Rabbi Shmelke.

On Sunday morning, Rabbi Shmelke convened the court, and invited Aharon to present the facts of the case. Rabbi Shmelke asked several questions, then sent Aharon outside while the judges deliberated. Soon a clerk called Aharon back into the courtroom.

Rabbi Shmelke looked up from a pile of open books and said, "After hearing the facts and consulting the relevant precedents in Jewish law, I am ready to issue a ruling. The court hereby rules that the wedding must take place as planned. I bless you, Aharon. May the couple be happy together, and may you merit to dance at your grandchildren's wedding."

Aharon sat in stunned silence.

"But Rebbe," he stammered, "How can you rule against me? On Friday you told me I was fortunate that I had come to you for a ruling!"

Rabbi Shmelke looked puzzled for a moment, then a look of compassion crossed his face.

"If I said something which you misinterpreted, I beg your forgiveness. I did not intend to mislead you. But you misunderstood my words. I told you on Friday that you are fortunate that you have come to me for a ruling. You are indeed fortunate that it is *you* coming to me with this predicament rather than the groom's parents; the groom's parents have lost their wealth while you still have yours. If the tables were turned, and the groom's parents were coming to me seeking to annul your children's wedding – then you would be truly unfortunate."

"As events have turned out," he concluded, "you are indeed fortunate to be faced with the dilemma of whether to carry on with the wedding. As for your daughter – do not be upset that she is marrying a poor boy. Rejoice instead in the fact that God has granted you the wealth to help them start their life together."

You Are Indeed Fortunate To Be Facing The Dilemmas That Come With Your Position

Rabbi Shmelke's perspective is as pertinent for managers as it is for affluent but skeptical in-laws. Yes, the work of management is full of problems, dilemmas, and painful decisions. Yes, managers bear the weight of great responsibility. And yet, never forget that you are indeed fortunate to be a manager. If you are shouldering managerial responsibility, it means you are earning a commensurate salary and have more challenges and privileges than the people whom you manage. It means you have earned the trust of your company to the point where you can influence decisions that can change the company's future. If you find the work of managing to be a burden, stop for a moment and consider its benefits.

In Today's World

A survey of over 4,000 executives performed by Jan Halper in 1988 led her to some startling conclusions. Most managers, she discovered, were silently miserable at jobs that, to outsiders, reeked of power and success. Senior executives commonly lamented the burdens of their work, and felt a need to change, to "get from here to there," but didn't know how.

Those who were introspective, who valued their logic and intuition, were able to deal with the stresses of management. However, "those who appeared outwardly successful, but ignored their inner life, were often confused, empty or discontented, which resulted in their feeling overwhelmed or depressed and caused them to run away from their problems." Accustomed to using external yardsticks to measure success, they "pass out scorecards to everyone but themselves, live their lives for everyone else," and use arrogance to cover up their own insecurities.[73]

An ever-growing number of employees are simply not interested in becoming managers, says *The Wall Street Journal*'s Timothy D. Schellhardt. 80% of the workshop participants of an Atlanta leadership development firm, Manchester Consulting, say they want nothing to do with management, a major shift from a decade ago when 70% hoped to become managers.

Supervising others has always been a difficult role to fill, but in the past, that stress was offset by expectations of financial reward and career mobility. In today's business environment, perceptions and career assumptions have changed.

- Management is viewed as an unstable position, as companies eliminate layers of coordinators in favor of workers who can develop and sell products. American Management Association surveys indicate that three middle managers are laid off for every one hired. Only 43% of mid-level managers questioned recently by International Survey Research Corporation of Chicago think they will have a job with their employer as long as they perform well, down from 72% in 1991.
- The salary gap between managers and employees has been shrinking. In many high-tech companies, technical experts already earn more than department managers.

- The "Dilbert Factor" is also at work. Scott Adams' popular cartoon character, along with many television sitcoms, routinely portrays managers as morons, evil or both. Who wants to take on a position where she risks being treated, de facto, as an evil moron?

Given all these factors, is it any wonder that a career in management has lost some of its luster?[74]

So, in the final analysis, why be a manager?

Many of the potential motivations are negative – a desire to order people around, a need for status, the ability to use inside information for personal gain. These give management a bad name and help feed "the Dilbert Factor."

Then what are the positive motivations? Leadership guru Stan Slap, author of *Bury My Heart at Conference Room B*, answers by distinguishing between management and leadership. Management, he says, "is typically a soulless and confusing job. You're expected to hire, train and motivate the very best talent when they're not around to be hired, you don't have the time to train them, and you don't have the tools to motivate them. You're expected to explain strategies to your people when those strategies haven't been fully explained to you and then use your own good name to represent them when they come and go without coherent explanation. And you're expected to constantly sell people on the value of change when that change clearly has no value to them whatsoever."

Leadership, says Slap, is something else entirely. Leaders develop a vision of a better way, based on the core values that they live on the job. They are able to communicate their vision clearly, consistently and passionately so that others want to embrace it. By sharing their vision and their commitment with employees, by showing them a concrete path to achieve the vision, leaders create the trust and faith that mobilizes followers to move toward a common objective.

The benefit to an individual of being a manager, according to Slap, is that it provides an opportunity to exercise leadership. Seen in this light, leadership is not a burden – it's a profoundly personal and inherently narcissistic way to achieve your vision and live out your personal values.[75]

Chapter Summary: Lessons in Developing People from the Hasidic Masters

Here is a recap of the lessons from the stories in this chapter.

Core Values

- The team instinctively looks beyond the values to which you pay lip service, and accurately reflects the real values that matter to management. *Your audience hears your words, but they imitate your values and actions.*
- Are you the master or the slave to your work? *The worthy man works for his living, while the unworthy man lives for his work.*
- Better the embarrassment of failure than the shame of dishonesty. *There's no shame in wearing a cabbage leaf for a hat, so long as you came by it honestly.*
- In business, some degree of falseness is unavoidable. *When people expect water in their milk, give them water in their milk.*

Coping With Failure

- It is impossible to completely avoid failure; the key is in persisting and benefiting from your mistakes until you succeed. *A single success can more than repay the price of many failures.*
- Try to ensure that all the mistakes in your organization are new mistakes. *Share what you know about the wrong path.*

Being a Leader

- Remember the limits of your jurisdiction, outside of which your status is irrelevant. *A leader is not a leader from every angle.*

- Arguing a logical position, the manager should not pull rank on other team members. *In matters of logic and preparation, the leader's opinion is no better than anyone else's.*
- Sometimes you must take the blame for errors you did not commit, sacrificing your own prestige for the long-term good of the organization. *A great leader takes responsibility for mistakes he did not make.*
- No matter how burdensome the role of manager seems, remember: *You are indeed fortunate to be facing the dilemmas that come with your position.*

CHAPTER 6
Managing
the Outside
World

Rabbi Ayzel Kharif was the Chief Rabbi of the town of Slonim. He earned a sufficient wage to support both his own family and the family of his son-in-law Yossel, a promising young Talmudic scholar.

Rabbi Ayzel once teased his son-in-law. "Tell me, Yossel, which of us is the Chief Rabbi of Slonim? We are both distinguished Talmudic scholars. We preach in the synagogue on the Sabbath with equal frequency. And we are both sustained by wages from the town elders. So tell me, which of us is the Rabbi of Slonim?"

"I confess, I am confused." Yossel smiled in amusement. "How can we tell which of us is the Rabbi?"

"Here is my advice," Rabbi Ayzel said. "Go to the marketplace and listen in on the conversations. The man they are gossiping about – he is the Rabbi."

"You need to recruit partners, people who can protect you from attacks and who can point out potentially fatal flaws in your strategy or initiative... You also need to keep the opposition close... Have coffee once a week with the people most dedicated to seeing you fail. But, while relationships with allies and opponents are essential, the people who will determine your success are often those in the middle, the uncommitted, who are nonetheless wary of your plans... You want to be sure that their general uneasiness doesn't evolve into a move to push you aside."[76]

- Ronald A. Heifitz and Martin Linsky

אHasidic Rebbe leads his disciples using skills such as charisma, empathy and active listening. To manage the outside world, however, the Rebbe faces different challenges that require a different set of skills. He must obey his teachers and the other leaders of the generation, and tread carefully when these giants clash. He must form relationships with his peers, fellow Rebbes who frequently engage in passionate arguments and unite into ad hoc alliances. He must fight the opponents to Hasidism, who will stop at nothing to discredit the Rebbe and steer potential followers away.

Let us see what we can learn from the Hasidic Rabbis about how to manage the outside world: handling politics, hiring consultants, conducting negotiations and dealing with competitors.

POLITICS

Lesson 34: Know When To Keep Your Opinion To Yourself

Does My Breath Smell Sweet?

Rabbi Israel of Rozhin and Rabbi Haim of Tsanz once had a disagreement. Arguments between Hasidic rabbis were not private affairs; other rabbis and their followers took sides. Rabbi Meir of Zhidikov, however, ordered his followers not to enter the fray, and explained the reason by way of a parable:

"The lion was King of the Jungle. To amuse himself one day, he stopped a passing wolf and demanded of him, 'Does my breath smell sweet?' The wolf winced at the lion's foul breath. The lion saw this and bellowed 'Well, answer me!'

'Perhaps chewing some cinnamon bark would help,' stammered the wolf.

'How dare you speak thus to the King of the Jungle?' roared the lion, and he ate the wolf.

The bear passed next. 'Does my breath smell sweet?' demanded the lion of him.

The bear saw the remains of the wolf, and decided on flattery as the best approach. 'Your breath, oh great lion, smells like the flowers of the field and the spices of the valley.'

'Liar!' roared the lion, and ate the bear.

Next the lion met a fox, and asked him 'Does my breath smell sweet?'

The fox, warily eying the evidence of recent carnage, decided that discretion was the better part of valor. 'Please forgive me, Your Majesty the King, but my nose has been stuffed up for three days and I am unable to smell a thing.'

'You truly are the wisest animal in the forest,' laughed the lion, and let the fox pass."

"So too," said Rabbi Meir, "in this bitter argument between two great lions of Torah, it is best for us to stand aside. Indeed, our senses are too dull and we are not worthy to offer an opinion. Only thus may we hope to be saved from both these lions."

When Lions Battle, Keep Your Nose Out Of It

When arguments occur in the workplace, it can be very tempting to take sides. As this story illustrates, in some arguments, especially political struggles between superiors, the wisest course is to stay on the sidelines.

In Today's World

Practitioners in all fields look for patterns – proven solutions to recurring problems. In their book *The Manager Pool: Patterns for Radical Leadership*[77], Don Olson and Carol Stimmel apply the concept of patterns to the area of management. Taking a page from Rabbi Meir, they recommend responding to office politics with what they call the "Switzerland" pattern.

For centuries Switzerland has been surrounded by powerful nations that frequently wage war on each other. Through it all, Switzerland has remained neutral, a reliable business partner that can be trusted to conduct business discreetly and impartially.

207

So, too, argue Olson and Stimmel, though taking sides in an organization can be tempting, it may prove very damaging. Their advice is to imitate the behavior pattern of Switzerland. Remain neutral, i.e., don't take sides, avoid company politics and don't spread gossip. You will develop a position of stature among your fellow workers for being objective, impartial and trustworthy. You are Switzerland. Like Rabbi Meir's fox, you can thus maintain effective relationships with all parties, and avoid being dragged into destructive battles.

Lesson 35: Cultivate Your Team's Reputation For Excellence

The Rebbe's Apples

A poor widow who made her living selling apples at a stand in the market once came for guidance to Rabbi Haim of Tsanz. The woman could not make ends meet on her income from the stand.

"Rebbe," she sighed, "here it is Thursday afternoon, and I have not even earned enough to buy bread and wine for the Sabbath."

"Does your apple stand not provide you with a living?" asked Rabbi Haim.

"People say my apples are bad, and no one buys from me," she replied.

Rabbi Haim rose from his chair. "Let us go to your stand. I wish to see this with my own eyes."

They walked through the marketplace to the widow's stand. Rabbi Haim picked up an apple and examined it closely. After a moment, he held up the apple and called out, "This apple is perfect! Who wishes to buy a wonderful apple from me?"

A crowd gathered round. The holy Rabbi Haim, the spiritual leader of the generation, was selling an apple! Why, it must be a special apple, infused with blessing! One man offered twice its worth, a woman offered three times, and soon the apple had sold for ten times its value.

Rabbi Haim picked up an apple in each hand and called out, "Who wishes to buy good apples?" Bedlam

209

broke out, as people argued over the privilege of purchasing apples directly from the Rebbe, and thrust coins at the widow without even counting them. Within a few minutes all the apples had been sold for many times their worth.

As the woman counted her money, Rabbi Haim turned to leave. "You see," he said to her, "the problem was not your apples – they are excellent. The problem was that people just didn't know how excellent they were."

Put Your Weight Behind Your Team's Wares

Look closely at the way in which Rabbi Haim chooses to help the widow. He could issue a directive to his followers, telling them to frequent her apple stand. But that would not help the woman in time for the upcoming Sabbath meal. So Rabbi Haim takes a more proactive approach. He has something the widow does not – his status in the community – and he uses this unique qualification to the widow's advantage. He throws the full weight of his personal prestige behind the widow. We can think of him as a pioneer in promoting products via celebrity endorsement.

Rabbi Haim does not need to replace the widow at her stand and return personally the next market day to sell apples – all it took to put her on her feet was an opportune and well-publicized one-time gesture. It is an association that will continue to work for her tomorrow and the day after that.

As a manager, you typically delegate authority to subordinates and try to give them enough space to do their jobs. Still, as Rabbi Haim's story illustrates, there are situations where your intervention is necessary, where you need to personally step in with the full power of your own prestige. A well-timed gesture that shows you are firmly behind your subordinate is often sufficient.

Part of good management is providing subordinates with the protection and endorsement they need to do their jobs. Consider it a marketing task to ensure that your subordinates' efforts and skills are properly appreciated. To paraphrase Rabbi Haim, the problem is not your subordinates – like the apples, they are excellent. The problem is that your managers and peers may need to hear a plug from you to make them aware of just how excellent your subordinates are.

In Today's World

Jack Welch, the legendary CEO of General Electric, was famous for swooping in and getting personally involved in the details of problems. This doesn't mean he spent his days in a lab. Welch, for example, personally shepherded along a research process that led to an almost tenfold improvement in the tubes that go into GE's X-ray and CAT scan machines.

Welch once heard complaints from customers that the GE tubes were averaging 25,000 scans, less than half the life of competing tubes. He responded by reaching deep into the organization and summoning Marc Ornetto, the general manager of European maintenance, to his office. Ornetto's marching orders were simple.

"Fix it!" Welch demanded. "I want 100,000 scans out of my tubes."

For the next four years, Ornetto faxed weekly progress reports directly to Welch. Back came detailed comments from Welch, some flattering, some demanding, some growling. Welch used the weight of his prestige to open doors and sidestep corporate bureaucracy, giving Ornetto direct access to relevant expertise and technology throughout GE.

The experience astonished Ornetto. "I was just running a little business here... and I was so amazed that he could find the time to read my reports and then even send me back notes," he said.

Welch's detailed involvement paid off. Ornetto's team created tubes that average 200,000 scans, an improvement that added $14 million in productivity benefits. It also sent a strong message to the entire GE organization that Welch was committed to success and willing to sweat the details required to get there.[78]

It is informative to compare Welch's style to that of Rabbi Haim. Both leaders personally step in and use the their prestige to help a subordinate succeed. But Welch and Ornetto have a traditional employer-to-employee relationship, with Welch judging and criticizing Ornetto's performance. This is in marked contrast to Rabbi Haim's readiness to reverse roles to help the widow and, in effect, become her assistant for a day.

A modern parallel to Rabbi Haim's management style is the philosophy of "servant leadership" expounded by Robert K. Greenleaf. According to Greenleaf, a great leader puts other people's needs, aspirations and interests above his own. A servant leader does not look for power over subordinates, but rather seeks ways to serve them: to free them from obstacles that interfere with their success, and to assist them in their personal growth.

The best test of this management style, says Greenleaf, is, "Do those served grow as persons? Do they, while being served, become healthier, wiser, freer, more autonomous, more likely themselves to become servants?"[79] Seen in this light, Rabbi Haim's willingness to become the widow's helper makes him a prototypical servant leader.

Another example of servant leadership is provided by Aaron Feuerstein, owner of Malden Mills Industries, a textile firm based in Malden, Massachusetts. In December of 1995, three of Malden Mills' four production facilities burned to the ground. On the Wednesday following the fire, 1,400 employees lined up for what they thought would be their last paycheck.

Instead, Feuerstein announced that he would continue to pay their salaries and health benefits for at least another thirty days, even though the mill was closed. Through sheer willpower, Feuerstein and his production crew managed to resume production in the remaining facility within ten days of the fire. When Feuerstein shook hands with every employee that day, they were crying tears of joy. One worker said, "Aaron, we're going to pay you back tenfold."

On January 12, 1996, Feuerstein shocked the media and his employees by announcing that he would pay his employees for still another thirty days, even though most of them were not yet back at work. These extra months of salary cost over $15 million. But, in the following months, thanks to the dedication of the employees, Malden Mills was able to recoup its losses and return to its pre-fire revenues, in what has become known as the "Malden Miracle."

CONSULTANTS

Lesson 36: Don't Assume A Consultant Has All The Answers

The Great Professor of Anipoli

Once there was a Hasid named Avraham whose wife fell seriously ill. Her condition worsened from day to day, and the local doctors were unable to cure her. Avraham traveled to Nishchiz to seek the counsel of his Rebbe, Rabbi Mordechai.

"Rebbe, I've come to ask you to help my wife," implored Avraham. "I have been unable to find a doctor who can cure her. Please counsel me – who is the best doctor to heal her?"

Rabbi Mordechai did not hesitate. "You should travel to the great Professor of Anipoli. He will cure your wife."

Avraham thanked the Rebbe, and immediately set out on horseback. The journey from Nishchiz to Anipoli was long and arduous. Avraham approached the first person he saw when he arrived in Anipoli.

"Can you please tell me where the great Professor lives?"

"We have no professor in this town," was the puzzled reply.

Avraham rushed to the town synagogue and asked an elderly gentleman, "Can you please tell me where the great Professor lives?"

The gentleman was mystified. "We have no professor in Anipoli," he responded kindly.

Avraham was undaunted. "Perhaps he is not known in these parts as Professor. Can you please tell me where the town doctor lives?"

"Anipoli is a very small town," said the old man, "so small that we don't even have a doctor here."

Avraham thought for a moment. "Perhaps he works as a pharmacist?"

Again the old man shook his head. "I'm afraid we do not even have a pharmacist in our town."

Avraham was stunned. His Rebbe was a holy man, with vast knowledge of this world and the world to come. How could Rabbi Mordechai have made such a grave error as to send him looking for the great Professor of Anipoli, a doctor who did not exist?

Full of doubt, Avraham made his way back to Nishchiz and came before Rabbi Mordechai. "I followed your advice and went to find the great Professor of Anipoli, but Anipoli has no professor! They don't even have a doctor or a pharmacist!"

"So, what does a person in Anipoli do when he falls ill?" asked Rabbi Mordechai.

"What can he do? What choice does he have?" blurted Avraham. "His only option is to pray to God to have mercy on him and send a cure from Heaven."

Rabbi Mordechai smiled. "Ah, yes. That is the great Professor of Anipoli I mentioned to you. And may He Who cures the people of Anipoli also bring your wife a speedy recovery."

And so it was. Avraham returned to his home and discovered that his wife's illness had passed.

There Is No Great Professor Of Anipoli

Avraham believes there must be a doctor somewhere who is greater than the local doctors. Rabbi Mordechai teaches him that his faith in some remote all-knowing shaman is misplaced.

Think of this story the next time you are tempted to hire a consultant. Is morale flagging in Engineering? Does the corporate network slow to a crawl every afternoon? Did an embarrassing bug sneak by the Quality Assurance department?

Never fear! There is an army of consultants eager to help you solve your company's problems. Each of them claims to be the great Professor of Anipoli, possessing knowledge and experience far beyond that available in your organization.

Before you rush out in search of an all-knowing consultant, consider the resources within your organization whose power can be brought to bear to research and address the problem. Perhaps a task force would allow you to share information from several areas and come up with a new perspective. Perhaps you suspect possible causes and probable solutions, but have never given high priority to diagnosing and resolving the problem.

Like Avraham, you may expend a great deal of time, effort and money seeking out the great Professor of Anipoli, only to discover that the Professor offers no better answer than the one that was under your nose all along.

In Today's World

Lou Gerstner, IBM's legendary CEO, had an insider's view of consulting, based on his experience as an ex-director of McKinsey. Consultants' "dirty little secret," revealed Gerstner, is that it is not hard to come up with attractive strategies in public markets where good information is readily available. The true differentiator is how you implement the strategies. And consultants cannot do that in your stead.[80]

Companies pay over $50 billion per year to advice-givers. Granted that some proportion of the advice seems to simply repeat back information you yourself provided. But in many instances, consultants do bring sophisticated expertise to clients, and provide a fresh outside perspective that ultimately improves the client company's bottom line.

There are innumerable examples of impressive results from successful consulting assignments. For example:

- A.T. Kearney & Co. helped Sears, Roebuck & Co. save millions by finding alternative sources for products such as auto batteries.
- Andersen Consulting helped Harley-Davidson Inc. to turn their business around, over the course of a decade, by cutting costs.
- Boston Consulting Group helped pharmaceutical manufacturer Boehringer Mannheim Group develop a strategy to successfully market a breakthrough medical device for diabetics.

On the other hand, though the successes far outnumber the failures, we often hear colorful reports of botched or wasteful consulting assignments:

- In the early 1990's, Cleveland-based Figgie International used consultants to improve their manufacturing capabilities, and nearly went bankrupt after racking up over $75 million in consulting fees.
- Between 1989 and 1994, AT&T spent nearly half a billion dollars on consultants with no defined goals or tangible results.
- Bain & Co. Inc.'s consulting relationship with Dublin-based Guiness PLC ended abruptly when the Bain

consultant turned state's evidence against his former clients, sending several of them to jail.

So hiring external advisors is clearly a double-edged sword. How can you know when to use consultants and how to use them wisely?

In the final analysis, perhaps the real danger to corporations comes not from the out-of-control consultant, but rather from the executive who abrogates managerial responsibility by blindly placing faith in the advice of external experts.

In their book *Dangerous Company: The Consulting Powerhouses and the Businesses They Save and Ruin*[81], James O'Shea and Charles Madigan say, "Good advice depends upon the shrewdness of the person who seeks it." They recommend that anyone hiring a consultant define clear and measurable goals, closely monitor progress, and retain control of the assignment. In other words, manage the consultant's assignment as you would any other assignment for which you are ultimately responsible. Don't drop the reins just because the work has been outsourced.

Although there may be no Great Professor of Anipoli, you can enjoy the advantages of using consultants by being realistic about the benefits they can provide and hardheaded about how to derive them. The Wizard of Oz may not have been a great wizard, but taken as a mere mortal he did a pretty solid job.

NEGOTIATIONS

Lesson 37: Know What The Other Side Values

Onions for Gold

Rabbi Jacob Kranc, the Magid of Dubno, once paid a call on a wealthy man who was known for his Torah erudition. The purpose of the visit was to raise funds for a charitable cause. Rabbi Jacob's intent, as was customary, was to deliver a 'word of Torah,' a short sermon to enlighten and entertain his host, and, in return, to receive a worthy contribution.

Imagine Rabbi Jacob's surprise when, after his 'word of Torah,' the rich man responded with his own 'word of Torah!' Rabbi Jacob, determined to collect money for his cause, delivered another short sermon, but his host again responded with a sermon of his own.

Rabbi Jacob smiled at his host.

"Let me tell you a parable," he said.

"Once a man was traveling at sea when a great storm arose and destroyed his boat. With the last of his strength, he swam to the shore of a desert island. All the man could save from the boat was a knapsack full of food.

The man discovered that a peaceful tribe inhabited the island. He noticed that gold was plentiful on the island, and therefore the natives considered it to be of little value. On the other hand, he observed that the island had a limited range of edible plants.

The man happened to have some onions in his knapsack, which the natives had never seen nor tasted. He planted the onions, and when they grew, he distributed them to the inhabitants, who found onions to be an excellent seasoning for their food. To express their gratitude, the natives filled the man's knapsack with gold.

Soon afterwards the man was rescued from the island and returned home. He told a friend the source of his new fortune, and the friend spotted a golden opportunity.

'If the natives liked onions, they'll love garlic,' he reasoned.

So he filled his knapsack with garlic and set out for the desert island. When he arrived, the garlic was indeed very well received. To express their gratitude, the natives rewarded the man by filling his knapsack with their most precious possession – onions!"

"The same is true of us," said Rabbi Jacob to the rich man. "When I provide you with words of Torah, you express your appreciation by giving me back words of Torah. But I do not need words of Torah from you – I need gold!"

Know What Your Negotiating Partner Values – Onions Or Gold

To succeed in negotiations, you must understand what is precious to the other side. In many cases, you will be amazed to discover that they do not equally value what is precious to you. You must strip away your own assumptions and biases, and look at the issues through your negotiating partner's eyes. Only then can you arrive at the optimal "win-win" resolution, where each side comes away with what it wants most.

In Today's World

In his article "Six Habits of Merely Effective Negotiators," James K. Sebenius provides an excellent example of "garlic for onions" mismatched assumptions.[82]

A company developed a technology for detecting leaks in underground gas tanks that was far cheaper and more accurate than competing products. The Environmental Protection Agency had recently mandated that these tanks be continuously tested. Sounds like perfect timing, doesn't it? And yet, the company failed to close a single sale.

The root of the failure lay in a misunderstanding of what the potential customer really valued. EPA regulations permitted leaks of up to 1500 gallons, while the new technology could detect leaks as small as 8 ounces. Installing such a device would only increase the customer's headaches, inviting needless and expensive regulatory attention. A potential buyer might wish for his competitor to have this product installed, but certainly had no interest in purchasing one himself.

At the other extreme, there are many cases of two companies arriving at "garlic for gold" win-win arrangements even though they are fierce competitors in other areas. Novell's Ray Noorda calls this unusual mix of cooperation and competition "coopetition." Some examples:

- Canon Inc. and Hewlett Packard go head-to-head in the inkjet printer market. Yet, Canon is a key supplier of printer engines for HP's laser printers.
- The Microsoft Network (MSN) and America On Line (AOL) are in direct competition for the hearts and eyes of the online community. Nonetheless, AOL carries Slate, Microsoft's online magazine, because it boosts readership on their site.

- Microsoft competes with Apple in the personal computer market, but also licenses its Office applications to Apple, and recently invested in this rival to the tune of $150 million.

Necessity can indeed be the mother of strange bedfellows.

Lesson 38: Look Past The Obvious To The Context

The Lame Traveler

A Hasid named Yosef once traveled from his home in Apta to visit his Master, Rabbi Israel, the Preacher of Kozhnitz. The way was long, and it took Yosef and his driver a week by horse and carriage to reach their destination.

As always, the days in Kozhnitz passed quickly, and all too soon the time came for Yosef to bid the Preacher farewell and receive a blessing for the trip back to Apta.

Rabbi Israel spoke with him about various matters, then asked, "Yosef, you travel a great distance to visit me, and I imagine you often pass travelers along the way who cannot afford a carriage and must make the long journey on foot. When such a poor sojourner asks to ride in your wagon, what do you do?"

"Whenever someone asks for a ride, I order my carriage driver to stop and help," replied Yosef with pride. "I always take the poor traveler safely to his destination."

"Very good," said the Preacher. "Now suppose you came across a lame traveler limping along on a cane, who asked to ride in your wagon. What would you do in such a situation?"

Yosef did not hesitate. "Why, of course I would stop and take such a traveler, who is suffering with every step of his journey."

The Preacher shook his head decisively. "Yosef, your empathy for your fellow man is admirable. But, in such a situation, I must warn you, under no circumstances should you stop for a lame traveler."

And with no further explanation, the Preacher bid Yosef goodbye.

Yosef was puzzled. Why had his Master chosen to discuss this question with him? And why should one not stop to help such a traveler? Perplexed, Yosef took his driver and set out on the long trip back to Apta.

Yosef lay in the back of the carriage and soon dozed off. Some time later, the wagon stopped and he awoke.

"Where are we?" he asked groggily.

"We are in the forest," replied the driver. "I just passed a lame man hobbling along on two canes. He begged me to stop and give him a ride. I know you take pity on such travelers, so I've pulled over and am waiting for the poor man to catch up with us."

Yosef awoke with a start. This was precisely the situation the Preacher had warned him against! Sitting up, Yosef looked back and saw a man dressed in rags, leaning on his canes as he limped slowly toward the wagon.

"Drive off as fast as you can! We must leave right now!" shouted Yosef to the startled driver.

The traveler neared the back of the carriage, and pleaded, "Please wait! Have mercy on me and let me ride in your wagon!"

The driver was paralyzed with confusion. Yosef grabbed away the reins and whipped the horses to urge them forward. The carriage slowly pulled away from the lame man. Glancing back over his shoulder, Yosef saw the traveler walk faster to catch the wagon. To Yosef's surprise, the man broke into a trot and then sprinted after them, but was unable to overtake the carriage. As the horses picked up speed, Yosef saw other men burst out of the forest to join the traveler, and they all shook their fists and cursed the receding carriage.

"That was not a lame man in need of help," he shouted to the driver, "it was an ambush of bandits! They intended to rob and kill us!"

Yosef was amazed by the prescience and wisdom of his Master Rabbi Israel.

When Yosef next traveled back to Kozhnitz, Rabbi Israel hugged him in greeting. "Yosef, I am pleased to see you are well and have traveled safely."

Yosef told the Preacher of his brush with danger.

"I am glad you followed my advice," said Rabbi Israel. "I received reports of this gang of thieves from other travelers, and I knew that you would have pity on a lame man, for your heart is often stronger than your head. Had you analyzed the situation rationally, you would have yourself realized the flaw in your judgment."

"A healthy man sets out on a long journey, trusting his legs to take him to his destination. If he gets a ride, all the better; if not, he walks the whole way."

"Not so a lame man who relies on a cane. Such a man would never dream of setting out on such a journey in the first place. How can he count on the kindness of other travelers in order to reach his destination? No, it is obvious that such a traveler is not lame at all – he is only pretending to be lame. His very appearance discloses his evil intent. Who knows what scheme such a charlatan has in store for you?"

> ## Beware The Lame Traveler, Who Has No Business Setting Out On A Long Journey In The First Place

When a traveler on foot requests a ride from a passing carriage, a subtle negotiation occurs. If handled correctly, the result can be a win-win situation: the traveler receives a welcome rest, and the carriage owner receives the satisfaction of having helped someone in need. If either side misreads the intentions of the other, however, the results can be disastrous.

Rabbi Israel offers an important insight that is useful in any negotiation: when evaluating the other side's stance, look beyond external appearances and stated positions, to the context that brought your negotiating partner to his current position. If this context is inconsistent with the stance he is presenting, if he appears to be a lame traveler in the midst of a long journey – beware of a bluff.

In Today's World

An episode from Theodore Roosevelt's 1912 election campaign illustrates how a partner to a negotiation can miss out when he ignores the negotiating context.

Running a close race with Woodrow Wilson, Roosevelt arranged a final whistle-stop tour, during which he intended to distribute an elegant pamphlet adorned by a suitably presidential portrait.

Only after three million copies of the pamphlet had been printed did a campaign worker notice the fine print under Roosevelt's photograph: "Moffet Studios, Chicago." Moffet held the copyright, and unauthorized use of the photo could cost the campaign up to a dollar per copy. Campaign workers saw that they were in a serious bind: there was no time to reprint the pamphlet, but the campaign could hardly afford to pay a three million dollar copyright fee. And the success of the campaign hinged on getting those pamphlets out to the public.

Dispirited, they brought the problem to the campaign manager, George Perkins. Perkins fired off a telegram to Moffet Studios: "We are planning to distribute millions of pamphlets with Roosevelt's picture on the cover. It will be great publicity for the studios whose photographs we use. How much will you pay us to use yours? Respond immediately."

Moffet responded, "We've never done this before, but under the circumstances we'd be pleased to offer you two hundred and fifty dollars."

Perkins graciously accepted the offer, and the pamphlets were distributed as planned.[83]

Perkins' misrepresentation raises a question of ethics. But his genius lay in his ability to successfully play the lame traveler, to hide from Moffet the true context of the negotiations. Conversely, Moffet did not ask enough questions. They believed the lame traveler and accepted the telegram at face value, rather than investigating the circumstances that had brought an election campaign to request rights to a pivotal photo at the eleventh hour.

Lesson 39: Sometimes Your Best Bet Is To Stall For Time

Playing for Time

The Prince of Shklov distinguished himself, even in the feudal society of eighteenth century Poland, for his malevolence and cruelty toward the Jewish subjects within his jurisdiction. He once assembled the Jews of the town and told them, "I am tired of hearing from your rabbis how wise you Jews are. If you are such a clever people – teach my dog to talk! I will be back in six months, and if my dog cannot talk by then, I shall expel all you Jews from my town!"

The Jews were dumbstruck. They waited for their communal leaders to plead with the Prince, but the leaders were paralyzed with fear. Suddenly from the back of the crowd, Nachum the Peddler spoke up. "I am prepared to fulfill the Prince's request, but six months is not enough time. I will need to have the dog in my house for five years in order to teach it to talk."

The Prince was amused. "Fine, I will give you five years. But be warned: if, after five years, the dog cannot talk, I will personally skin you alive." With that, the Prince gave Nachum the dog and left.

The Jews of Shklov were amazed by Nachum's offer.

The Rabbi asked Nachum, "Do you have any hope of teaching this dog to talk within five years? What will you do when the five years are up? We'll all be expelled, and you'll be killed!"

"May God be with us!" shrugged Nachum. "Five years is a long time. During those five years, perhaps the Prince will die, perhaps the dog will die, perhaps they both will die. And in five years, who knows? The dog might even learn how to talk!"

> ## Sometimes Your Best Bet Is To Wait For The Prince To Die

When there are no good options on the table, the best possible way to handle a negotiation is to buy time. As Will Rogers once said, "Diplomacy is the art of saying 'nice doggie' while you feel around for a bigger stick."

In Today's World

Microsoft recently put Nachum's tactics to effective use in the anti-trust case brought against it by the United States Department of Justice.

In November of 1999, after two years of hearings, Judge Thomas Penfield Jackson ruled that Microsoft held monopolistic power and had used it to harm consumers, rivals and other companies. For example, Microsoft was accused of shutting the competing browser, Netscape Navigator, out of the market by designing its Windows operating system to favor its own browser, Internet Explorer. To destroy the monopoly, Judge Jackson decreed that Microsoft should be split into two companies.

In response, Microsoft began a long and tortuous appeal process, filing briefs four times the usual length and requesting a timetable with six months between hearings. Microsoft used these stalling tactics to great advantage.

- As long as the appeal process continued, Microsoft was free to continue to drive sales using monopolistic practices.
- The stalling tactics bought Microsoft enough time to launch its new Windows XP operating system. Windows XP integrated Internet services, such as instant messaging, even deeper into the operating system, allowing Microsoft to control the Internet browser as comprehensively as it already controlled the computer desktop.
- Microsoft was able to stall until George W. Bush was elected President. Bush, who was very supportive of Microsoft, quickly moved to have the case dropped.

In September 2001 the Justice Department ruled that it no longer sought to break up Microsoft, and negotiated a quick and – for Microsoft – relatively painless settlement. Ultimately, Microsoft outlasted the Prince.

COMPETITORS

Lesson 40: What Goes Around Comes Around

Muddying the Waters

Rabbi Meir of Premishlan once received a visit from a Hasid who came for advice about his business problems.

"I own a store that has provided my family with a good living for many years. Then, a year ago, a competing store opened up right across the street! Since then, I've lost a lot of business, and I can barely support my family. Rabbi Meir, please pray to God on my behalf that the other store should fail!"

Rabbi Meir paused for a moment, as if lost in thought, then asked, "Tell me, have you ever noticed how a horse drinks water from a stream?"

The Hasid was puzzled. "No, how?"

Rabbi Meir continued, "The horse first kicks its hooves in the stream, and only then begins to drink. Do you know why the horse stirs up the water first?"

"No, why?" the Hasid asked.

"I will explain it to you," said Rabbi Meir. "When the horse first looks into the stream, it sees its own reflection. The horse does not understand that it is looking at itself, and thinks another horse has come to drink its water. The horse therefore kicks at the stream, to frighten the other horse away. Of course, we know how pointless this is – there is really no other horse there, and even if there were, there is more than enough water in the stream for both. All the horse accomplishes is to muddy its own drinking water."

The Hasid left, chastened by Rabbi Meir's reprimand.

Don't Muddy Your Own Drinking Water

Like the Hasid in the story, many companies react to competitors by wishing them harm or by actively seeking ways to hasten their demise. But, as Rabbi Meir astutely points out, a company engaged in such negative activity and dirty pool (pun intended) pollutes the environment for the entire industry, and ultimately inflicts as much damage on itself as on its competitors.

In Today's World

Until 1911, wooden matches were made using white phosphorus. This substance caused necrosis, a dread disease that was often fatal to match plant workers. Chemists of the Diamond Match Company were able to replace the toxic white phosphorus with chlorate of potash, thereby creating the first safe, nonpoisonous match. In 1911, Diamond Match patented their technique. They were on the verge of an enormous money-maker.

In light of public health concerns, President William Howard Taft asked the company to voluntarily surrender its patent rights. Despite the loss of huge potential profits, Diamond agreed to surrender the patent, and even went so far as to send representatives to other match factories to teach them how to make nonpoisonous matches.

Diamond has managed to combine ethics with profitability. Diamond Brands Inc. continues to thrive today. Not only are they still a leading brand in matches, they have added many additional products to their line – plastic cutlery, toothpicks and other household goods.

If Microsoft's Bill Gates were to join the team of contestants on the "Survivor" TV series, he would have excellent chances of winning. Microsoft has proven itself to be a master at building alliances with business partners, only to turn on them later, cornering their markets or pressuring them not to do business with rivals. For example, in their efforts to control the Internet browser market, Microsoft was accused of demanding that hardware vendors dependent on Microsoft's Windows operating system snub the competing browser from Netscape.

Microsoft's "take no captives" approach partially explains its dominant position in the personal computer space. But this market is reaching saturation, as evidenced by flat hardware sales and a dwindling number of reasons for users to upgrade their existing software. To survive, the company will have to find new and diverse markets.

Microsoft has already spent billions of dollars in an effort to gain footholds in potential new markets: interactive television, game stations, online content and toys. To date, these efforts have failed. Many analysts report a common reason for Microsoft's impasse in these markets: a failure to form the partnerships needed to establish the company's presence in these new areas.

In the cable television industry, potential business partners are quoted as saying that Microsoft's record in the PC industry indicates that the company is not trustworthy. In the telephony space, Dwight Davis of Summit Strategies observes, "[Microsoft's] methods of operation have often been 'take no prisoners'. The telephone companies and the handset manufacturers are certain they don't want this fate to befall them."[84]

It seems that, by employing aggressive methods like those of the horse in Rabbi Meir's parable, Microsoft may have muddied its own drinking water.

Chapter Summary: Lessons in Managing the Outside World from the Hasidic Masters

Here is a recap of the lessons from the stories in this chapter.

Politics

- *When lions battle, keep your nose out of it.* Your best response to a political battle between superiors is to emulate Switzerland – adopt neutrality.
- Sometimes you need to personally step in to provide subordinates with the protection and endorsement they need to do their jobs. *Put your weight behind your team's wares.*

Consultants

- *There is no Great Professor of Anipoli.* The array of expert consultants eager to help you solve your problems may have no better solution than one you and your team can devise yourselves.

Negotiations

- *Know what your negotiating partner values – onions or gold.* Strip away your own assumptions and biases to look through the other side's eyes.
- *Beware the lame traveler, who has no business setting out on a long journey in the first place.* Look beyond external appearances and the stated positions of your negotiating partner for insight into the context that brought him to his current position.
- When there are no good options on the table, play for time. *Sometimes your best bet is to wait for the Prince to die.*

Competitors

- *Don't muddy your own drinking water.* Playing dirty pool pollutes the environment for everyone, and ultimately inflicts as much damage on you as on your competition.

CONCLUSION

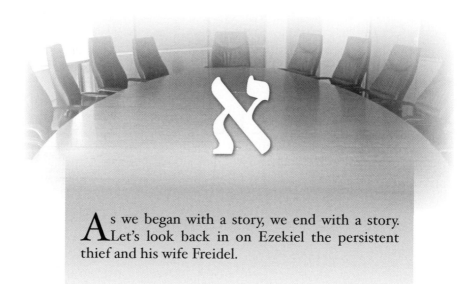

As we began with a story, we end with a story. Let's look back in on Ezekiel the persistent thief and his wife Freidel.

Although he did not usually lead the prayer services, Rabbi Moshe Leib of Sasov always led the Selichot, the penitential prayers recited on the eve of Yom Kippur, the Day of Atonement. His sweet voice moved the congregation to tears and to repentance.

One year, Rabbi Moshe Leib was late for the penitential prayers. The congregation waited patiently for half an hour, then they sent the caretaker to find their Rabbi. The caretaker searched everywhere – in Rabbi Moshe Leib's study, in the ritual bath, on the streets of the city – but Rabbi Moshe Leib was nowhere to be found. After several hours of searching, the caretaker stood bewildered outside the door of Rabbi Moshe Leib's study, wondering what had become of the rabbi. Suddenly, the door opened, and out walked – Rabbi Moshe Leib!

Without a word of explanation, the rabbi strode to the synagogue and began chanting the penitential prayer. After the service, the congregants asked the caretaker where Rabbi Moshe Leib had been. The caretaker had no rational explanation. "I searched for him everywhere. I was certain he wasn't in his room, and then he suddenly appeared. He must have gone to Heaven!"

The next year and the year after that, Rabbi Moshe Leib was again nowhere to be found until he emerged from his room to lead the penitential prayers. It soon became a matter of common knowledge among Rabbi Moshe Leib's followers, who believed with complete faith that each year, before the penitential prayers, their rabbi ascended to Heaven to pray for forgiveness on behalf of his congregation.

One year a student of Rabbi Moshe Leib's named Zvi Hirsch of Zhidikov came to visit his master for the High Holidays. Zvi decided that he wanted to learn the secret of his rabbi's ascension to Heaven. So, before the eve of the penitential prayers, Zvi hid himself under the bed in Rabbi Moshe Leib's study and waited quietly.

A few hours later, Zvi heard the door open and saw Rabbi Moshe Leib enter the room. The Rabbi went to the closet and took out a coarse woolen cap, tattered pants and clumsy boots. After donning these clothes, the rabbi looked like a peasant. Rabbi Moshe Leib then climbed on the bookcase, up to the window, and, to Zvi's surprise, jumped out into the street! Zvi quickly crawled out of his hiding place and went outside. Intent on learning his Master's ways, he followed Rabbi Moshe Leib, trying not to reveal his presence.

Rabbi Moshe Leib strode to the home of Ezekiel the Thief, and knocked loudly on the door.

"It's Ignatz!" he shouted gruffly, sounding to Zvi like a Polish peasant. "Is Ezekiel home?"

From inside the house came the response of Ezekiel's wife Freidel. "Ezekiel was arrested two weeks ago! Now please go away – I have nothing to offer you. I am ill, my children are crying from the cold, and I have no wood for the fire."

Zvi followed Rabbi Moshe Leib into the forest. The Rabbi found a dry tree, took an axe from his pocket, and began chopping. Soon there was a pile of wood, which Rabbi Moshe Leib tied into a bundle and carried back to Ezekiel's home. He banged on the door and shouted, "It's Ignatz. I have some wood that I cannot sell. Please take the wood before it gets wet and use it – you can pay me later."

Freidel opened the door. "But I don't know how to stoke the oven," she said weakly.

"Let me start the fire," said Ignatz. "I need to warm myself up."

From outside, Zvi soon heard the sound of a fire crackling in the oven.

"Now I want something hot to drink," demanded Ignatz.

"I'm too ill to get up and prepare you anything," apologized Freidel.

"Then I will make a hot drink for both of us," said Ignatz. Soon Freidel was enjoying a cup of hot tea.

"The noise of the children is bothering me," declared Ignatz.

"I'm sorry," said Freidel, "but I am bedridden and cannot get up to calm them."

"Then I will quiet them," said Ignatz. Soon the children were asleep in their beds.

Zvi saw 'Ignatz' leave Freidel and Ezekiel's home and climb back into the window of his study. Zvi went to the synagogue, and soon Rabbi Moshe Leib appeared to lead the congregation. After the service, the congregants surrounded Zvi.

"So, does Rabbi Moshe Leib really go up to Heaven before the penitential prayers?" they asked.

"Yes, he goes up to Heaven," answered Zvi, "if not higher."

א

Rabbi Moshe Leib could have gone up to Heaven if he so desired, simply by living the pure and spiritual life of a Hasidic Rabbi, isolated from the outside world. But as 'Ignatz' the peasant, by personally performing good deeds and humbly and anonymously assisting those who most needed his help, Rabbi Moshe Leib went even higher, and brought some of Heaven down to this earth.

This story captures the essence of The Hasidic Masters' Guide to Management. Rabbi Moshe Leib is not a mystic in the most common sense of the word – he does not leave this world to dwell in another. Rather, he is what Rabbinic scholar Max Kadushin refers to as a "normal mystic," who seeks to bring the Divine into all the mundane activities of this world.

We managers can take a page from Rabbi Leib's book. It's easy enough to "go up to Heaven," to live a lofty and ethical personal life outside of work, away from the issues and conflicts of your job. To go even higher, you must look for ways to bring your values to bear on the world of business. By doing so, you can bring a bit of Heaven down here to earth, to yourself, your team and your company.

Notes

Introduction

[1] Anaïs Nin, *The Diary of Anaïs Nin*, Harvest Books, 1975.

[2] Peter F. Drucker, *The Practice of Management*, Harper & Row Publishers, 1986.

[3] Gerald A. Michaelson, *Sun Tzu: The Art of War for Managers*, Adams Media, 2001.

[4] Wess Roberts, *Leadership Secrets of Attila the Hun*, Warner Publishing, 1990.

[5] Gerald R. Griffin, *Machiavelli on Management: Playing and Winning the Corporate Power Game*, Praeger Publishers, 1991.

Chapter 1: Motivating and Communicating

[6] Peter F. Drucker, *The Practice of Management*, Harper & Row Publishers, 1986, p. 343.

[7] J. Sterling Livingston, "Pygmalion in Management", *Harvard Business Review*, January 2002.

[8] ibid.

[9] Dennis N.T. Perkins, *Leading at the Edge: Leadership Lessons from the Extraordinary Saga of Shackleton's Antarctic Expedition*, AMACOM Publishing, May 2000.

[10] Doris Kearns Goodwin, "Lessons of Presidential Leadership", *Leader to Leader*, No. 9, Summer 1998.

[11] Kathy McKimmie, "Serious Play", *Indiana Business Magazine*, August 3, 2003.

[12] Jim Thomas, "For team that defies physics, only Max Q will do", *St. Louis Post-Dispatch*, Feb. 1, 2002.

[13] Charles O'Reilly and Jeffrey Pfeffer, *Hidden Value: How Great Companies Achieve Extraordinary Results with Ordinary People*, Harvard Business School Press, August 2000.

[14] Annette Simmons, *The Story Factor: Inspiration, Influence and Persuasion through Storytelling*, Perseus Publishing, 2002.

[15] Noel M. Tichy, *The Leadership Engine*, HarperBusiness, 2002.

[16] Gary Klein, *Sources of Power: How People Make Decisions,* MIT Press, 1998.

[17] Mark Hurst, "Interview: Marissa Mayer, Product Manager, Google", goodexperience.com, October 15, 2002.

Chapter 2: Setting Objectives

[18] Peter F. Drucker, *The Practice of Management*, Harper & Row Publishers, 1986, p. 343.

[19] Ronald A. Heifitz and Marty Linsky, "A Survival Guide for Leaders", *Harvard Business Review*, June 2002.

[20] Jim Collins, *Good To Great: Why Some Companies Make the Leap...and Others Don't,* HarperCollins, 2001.

[21] ibid.

[22] Louis V. Gerstner, "Jump Starting Innovation: Government, Universities & Entrepreneurs", North Carolina State University, February 10, 2003.

[23] Douglas K. Smith and Robert C. Alexander, *Fumbling the Future: How Xerox Invented, then Ignored, the First Personal Computer*, Author's Choice Press, May 1999.

[24] "Flying High", Wharton Entrepreneurial Programs, Summer 2003.

[25] "Chrysler's Disciplined 'Pizzazz'", *The Globalist*, April 10, 2002.

[26] "AOL Time Warner: Deploy and Commoditize: Finding the sense of the deal", *The Motley Fool*, February 9, 2000.

[27] Hewlett-Packard press release, September 2001.

[28] Alissa Wilkinson, *Pepsi and Coke: The Battle Between Colas*, University of Iowa, December 1998.

[29] Barbara Mikkelson, "Knew Coke", snopes.com Urban Legends Reference Pages, May 1999.

[30] ibid.

[31] Nigel Nicholson, "How to Motivate Your Problem People", *Harvard Business Review*, January 2003.

[32] ibid.

[33] I am grateful to Human Resources consultant Yael Burla for this insight.

Chapter 3: Organizing the Group

[34] Peter F. Drucker, *The Practice of Management*, Harper & Row Publishers, 1986, p. 344.

[35] Beverly Kaye and Sharon Jordan-Evans, *Love 'Em Or Lose 'Em: Getting Good People to Stay*, Berret-Koehler Press, 1999.

[36] Stephen C. Lunden, *Fish! A Remarkable Way To Boost Morale and Improve Results,* Hyperion Press, March 2000.

[37] William Poundstone, *How Would You Move Mount Fuji?,* Little, Brown and Co., 2003.

[38] Joel Spolsky, "The Guerrilla Guide to Interviewing", www.joelonsoftware.com.

[39] Jack Welch and John Byrne, *Jack: Straight From The Gut*, Warner Books, 2001.

[40] ibid.

[41] Charles Kenney, *Riding the Runaway Horse: The Rise and Decline of Wang Laboratories,* Little Brown and Company, 1992.

[42] Joseph Weber and Louis Lavelle, "Family, Inc.", *BusinessWeek,* November 10, 2003.

[43] Malcolm Gladwell, "The Talent Myth", *The New Yorker,* July 22, 2002.

[44] Jeffrey Pfeffer, "Business and the Spirit: Management Practices that Sustain Values", Stanford University Research Paper No. 1713, October 2001.

[45] Debra Meyerson, "Everyday Leaders: The Power of Difference", *Leader to Leader*, Winter 2002.

[46] Steven Levy, *CRYPTO*, Viking Press, 2000.

[47] Jeffrey Pfeffer, "The Real Keys to High Performance", *Leader to Leader,* No. 8, Spring 1998.

Chapter 4: Measuring Performance

[48] Peter F. Drucker, *The Practice of Management*, Harper & Row Publishers, 1986, p. 344.

[49] Lesley Stones, "Quality Upstaged By Deadlines", *Business Day,* November 20, 2003.

[50]Jim Collins, "It's Time to Rethink the Silicon Valley Paradigm", *Red Herring Magazine,* July 1993.

[51] Douglas McGregor, *The Human Side of Enterprise*, McGraw-Hill, June 1985.

[52] "Dick Drew and the invention of masking tape", 3M Worldwide Web site, http://www.3m.com/about3m/pioneers/drew.jhtml.

[53] William Glanz, "NASA ignored dangers to shuttle, panel says", *The Washington Times*, August 27, 2003.

Chapter 5: Developing People

[54] Peter F. Drucker, *The Practice of Management*, Harper & Row Publishers, 1986, p. 344.

[55] Gregory Zuckerman, "Gutfreund, 'King of the Street', Returns in Less Exalted Position", *The Wall Street Journal*, November 14, 2001.

[56] "Business and the Spirit: Management Practices that Sustain Values", Jeffrey Pfeffer, Stanford University Research Paper No. 1713, October 2001.

[57] "Who Says CEO's Can't Find Inner Peace?", *BusinessWeek*, September 1, 2003.

[58] Mark Maremont, Jesse Eisinger and John Carreyrou, "How High Tech Dream Shattered in Scandal at Lernout & Hauspie", *The Wall Street Journal,* December 7, 2000.

[59] Steve Johnson, *Solve It, Don't Sell It*, Johnson Publishing Company, October 2002.

[60] Jon Entine and Martha Nichols, "Blowing the Whistle On Meaningless 'Good Intentions'", *Chicago Tribune*, June 20, 1996.

[61] Hanna Rosin, "The Evil Empire: The Scoop on Ben & Jerry's Crunchy Capitalism", *The New Republic*, September 1995.

[62] Anne Dearing, Robert Dilts and Julian Russel, "Leadership Cults and Cultures", *Leader to Leader,* Spring 2003.

[63] Jim Collins, "It's Time to Rethink the Silicon Valley Paradigm", *Red Herring Magazine,* July 1993.

[64] Nina Munk, "Steve Case's Last Stand", *Vanity Fair,* January 2003.

[65] John Micklethwait, "The Valley of Money's Delight", *The Economist*, March 29, 1997.

[66] Michael S. Malone, "John Doerr's Startup Manual", *Fast Company,* February 1997.

[67] Warren G. Bennis and Robert J. Thomas, *Geeks and Geezers: How Era, Values, and Defining Moments Shape Leaders,* Harvard Business School Press, 2002.

[68] Henry Mintzberg, "Managing Quietly", *Leader to Leader,* Spring 1999.

[69] Ronald A. Heifitz and Marty Linsky, *Leadership on the Line,* Harvard Business School Press, 2002.

[70] Max DuPree, *Leadership Is an Art,* Doubleday, New York, 1989, p. 9.

[71] Peter Wyden, *Bay of Pigs: The Untold Story,* Simon & Schuster, 1979.

[72] Barry Maher, "The Blame Game", from *Filling the Glass: The Skeptic's Guide to Positive Thinking in Business,* Dearborn Trade Publishing, January 2001.

[73] Jan Halper, *Quiet Desperation: The Truth about Successful Men,* Warner Books, 1988.

[74] Timothy D. Schellhardt, "Want To Be a Manager? Many People Say No, Calling Job Miserable", *The Wall Street Journal,* April 4, 1997.

[75] Stan Slap, *Bury My Heart at Conference Room B,* HarperCollins, New York, 2004.

Chapter 6: Managing the Outside World

[76] Ronald A. Heifitz and Marty Linsky, "A Survival Guide for Leaders", *Harvard Business Review,* June 2002.

[77] Don Sherwood Olson and Carol L. Stimmel, *The Manager Pool: Patterns for Radical Leadership,* Addison-Wesley 2001.

[78] John A. Byrne, "How Jack Welch Runs GE", *BusinessWeek,* June 8, 1998.

[79] Robert K. Greenleaf, *Servant Leadership: A Journey into the Nature of Legitimate Power and Greatness,* Paulist Press, November 2002.

[80] Louis V. Gerstner Jr, from a speech at the 2003 Emerging Issues Forum, Institute for Emerging Issues, North Carolina State University, February 10, 2003.

[81] James O'Shea and Charles Madigan, *Dangerous Company: The Consulting Powerhouses and the Businesses They Save and Ruin,* Penguin USA, September 1998.

[82] James K. Sebenius, "Six Habits of Merely Effective Negotiators", *Harvard Business Review*, April 2001.

[83] ibid.

[84] Frank Catalano, "Redefining Microsoft", *Seattle Weekly*, July 23, 2003.

BIBLIOGRAPHY

The Hasidic Masters held divergent views on many issues. The selection of stories in this book and my analysis of them ultimately reflect my own personal philosophy. Not all the stories in this volume were even told by Hasidic rabbis. For example, Rabbi Ezekiel Landau, who features in two of the stories retold here, was a staunch opponent of the Hasidic movement. In fact, he once ordered the burning of books written by some of the Rebbes whose Hasidic stories I retell in this volume. Hasidism has proven itself in the years since then to be a valuable contributor to Jewish life, rather than a heretical movement, so it seems a fitting rapprochement to include his stories in this collection.

I have been collecting and telling Hasidic stories for years, and the tales in this book are culled from my personal library. The stories originally appeared in classic Hebrew texts published a hundred years ago or more. Since then, they have been widely anthologized in Hebrew. Many of them have never appeared in English. I have re-told these stories, rather than translating any single version, and have taken some liberties where necessary to make the stories more suitable to the 21st century business audience.

I apologize to my readers for the fact that women are not equally represented in the Hasidic stories, or even in Drucker's definition of management roles. Both are the product of their respective eras and, as such, pre-dated the raised consciousness of our own era.

If you are interested in reading more Hasidic stories in English, you will enjoy the following books:

1. *Stories Within Stories from the Jewish Oral Tradition*, retold by Peninah Schram, Jason Aronson, Inc., Northvale, NJ, 2000

2. *The Magid of Dubno and his Parables*, by Benno Heinemann, Feldheim Publishing, Jerusalem, 1978

3. *The Great Hasidic Masters*, by Avraham Yaakov Finkel, Jason Aronson, Inc., Northvale, NJ, 1996

4. *Tales of the Hasidim: The Early Masters*, by Martin Buber, Schocken Books, New York, 1970

5. *Tales of the Hasidim: The Later Masters*, by Martin Buber, Schocken Books, New York, 1970

6. *The Hasidic Anthology: Tales and Teachings of the Hasidim*, by Louis I. Newman, Bloch Publishing Company, New York, 1944

7. *Hasidic Stories*, by Meyer Levin, Greenfield Ltd., Tel Aviv, 1978

8. *Tales of the Gaonim (Sages)*, by Rabbi Sholom Klass, The Jewish Press, Brooklyn, NY, 1967

9. *Legends of the Hasidim: An Introduction to Hasidic Culture and Oral Tradition in the New World*, by Jerome R. Mintz, The University of Chicago Press, Chicago, 1974

10. *The Thirteen Stories of Rabbi Nachman of Breslav*, translated by Ester Koenig, Hillel Press, Jerusalem, 1978

I also highly recommend the following Hebrew books:

1. *Sefer HaMa'asiyot* (The Book of Stories), 6 volumes, by Mordechai Ben Yekhezkiel, Dvir Publishing, Tel Aviv, 1977

2. *MeDor L'Dor* (From Generation To Generation), 6 volumes, by M. Lipson, Achiasaf Publishing, Tel Aviv, 1968

3. *Sarei HaMei'ah* (Princes of the Century), 6 volumes, by Rabbi Yehuda Leib Maimon, Mossad HaRav Kook, Jerusalem, 1990

4. *Be'er HaHasidut* (The Fountain of Hasidism), 10 volumes, by Eliezer Steinman, Knesset Publishing, Tel Aviv, 1960

5. *Sipurei Hasidim* (Hasidic Stories), 2 volumes, by Rabbi Shlomo Yosef Zevin, Bet Hillel Publishing, Jerusalem, 1956

6. *Hasidim V'Anshei Ma'aseh* (Hasidim and Men of Great Deeds), 2 volumes, by Eliyahu KiTov, Yad Eliyahu KiTov Publishing, Jerusalem, 1997

7. *Sipurei Hasidim* (Hasidic Stories), by Simkha Raz, Kol Mevaser Publishing, Mevasseret Zion, Israel, 2000

BIOGRAPHIES OF THE RABBIS MENTIONED IN THIS BOOK

Rabbi Abraham Jacob of Sadigora (1819-1883) was the son of Rabbi Israel of Rozhin.

Rabbi Dov Baer of Mezritch (1704-1772). After the Ba'al Shem Tov's death, he became the leader of the movement and spread Hasidism throughout Europe.

Rabbi Elimelekh of Lizhensk (1717-1787). An ascetic, he and his brother, Rabbi Zusia, spent years wandering from town to town to express their identification with the exile of the Divine Presence from Jerusalem.

Rabbi Haim of Tsanz (1793-1876). Known for his strictness in matters of learning and observance, he conducted his court modestly, eschewing the splendor of other Hasidic dynasties.

Rabbi Haim of Volozhin (1749-1821). Acknowledged leader of non-Hasidic Russian Jews. He founded a renowned Talmudic academy in Volozhin that became the prototype for European Jewish education.

Rabbi Isaac of Volozhin (d. 1849) succeeded his father Rabbi Haim as head of the rabbinic academy of Volozhin. He took an active role in communal affairs and represented the Jewish community to the Russian government.

Rabbi Isaac of Vorka (1799-1848). A disciple of Rabbi Simcha Bunim of P'shischa, he was known for his love of all Jews.

Rabbi Israel of Kozhnitz (1733-1814). An eloquent speaker, he was known as "The Preacher of Kozhnitz."

Rabbi Israel of Rozhin (1797-1850). The great grandson of Rabbi Dov Baer of Mezritch, he was the preeminent Hasidic leader of his generation. He established a grand "court" where he lived in great splendor and attracted thousands of followers.

Rabbi Israel the Son of Eliezer (1698-1760). The founder of the Hasidic movement, he was called the Ba'al Shem Tov (Master of the Good Name) because of his skill in using God's name in amulets to bring health and good fortune.

Rabbi Jacob Joseph of Polnau (1710-1782). The first theoretician of Hasidism and the first to collect the teachings of the Ba'al Shem Tov into a book.

Rabbi Joshua of Kotna (1820-1893) was one of the early rabbinic supporters of Zionism. He was on good terms with the Hasidim, especially Rabbi Yitzhak Meir of Gur.

Rabbi Ayzel Kharif (d. 1873). A Rabbi and Talmudic scholar known for his sharp wit.

Rabbi Jacob Kranc (pronounced *Krantz*) (1741-1804). The Magid (Preacher) of Dubno, he was known for his insightful parables.

Rabbi Ezekiel Landau (1713-1793). The preeminent Jewish authority of the 18th century, he served as the Chief Rabbi of Prague for almost forty years. He was a staunch opponent of Hasidism, and is reputed to have ordered the burning of the first Hasidic book written by Rabbi Jacob Joseph of Polnau.

Rabbi Levi Yitzhak of Berditchev (1740-1810). He stressed the element of joy in worship, and took it upon himself to defend the Jewish people before God.

Rabbi Isaac Luria (1534-1572). Leading Jewish mystic of the 16th century, he established an academy in Safed, Israel.

Rabbi Meir of Premishlan (1780-1850). A contemporary and friend of Rabbi Israel of Rozhin, he was known for performing miracles to assist his followers.

Rabbi Menachem Mendel of Kotsk (1787-1859) sought to develop an elite cadre of followers who would change the world through their absolute devotion to truth and spirituality. When this endeavor failed, Rabbi Menachem withdrew from the world and, for the last twenty years of his life, locked himself in a room off his study hall.

Rabbi Menachem Mendel of Lubavitch (1789-1866). Grandson of Rabbi Shneur Zalman of Liadi, he succeeded his father-in-law as the Lubavitcher Rebbe. Known as the Tzemach Tzedek, he worked tirelessly for the good of Russian Jews, even at great personal risk.

Rabbi Mordechai of Chernobyl (d. 1837) led the Hasidic dynasty founded by his father, Rabbi Nachum of Chernobyl.

Rabbi Mordechai of Nishchiz (1742-1800). One of the most famous miracle workers of his generation.

Rabbi Moshe Lev of Sasov (1745-1807). He was known for his charitable works and his love for all Jews.

Rabbi Moshe Zvi of Sevarin (d. 1838). He was known for his staunch opposition to the teachings of Rabbi Nachman of Breslav.

Rabbi Nachman of Breslav (1772-1811). The great-grandson of the Ba'al Shem Tov, he founded a school of Hasidism that emphasized prayer as a form of dialogue with God. He expressed many of his teachings in elaborate mystical tales.

Rabbi Naftali of Ropshitz (1769-1827). A student of Rabbi Elimelekh of Lizhensk, he is known for his pithy insights and sharp wit.

Rabbi Israel Salanter (1810-1883). Founder of the Musar (ethics) revival movement among non-Hasidic Jews, which stressed the importance of treating one's fellow man with kindness and respect.

Rabbi Samuel The Prince (993-1055). Vizier of Grenada, statesman, poet and scholar. His career marks the high point of Jewish life in Muslim Spain.

Rabbi Shalom Dov Baer of Lubavitch (1866-1920). Grandson of Rabbi Menachem Mendel of Lubavitch. He established a network of Jewish schools in Russia.

Rabbi Shmelke of Nicholsburg (1726-1778). He spread Hasidism to Moravia, where he established a major rabbinic academy.

Rabbi Shneur Zalman Of Liadi (1745-1813). He founded the Habad-Lubavitch dynasty, which stressed the scholarly aspects of Hasidism.

Rabbi Simcha Bunim of P'shischa (1765-1827) worked as a clerk in a timber firm and as a pharmacist before becoming a Hasidic Rebbe. He opposed the external trappings of the Hasidic life style and encouraged full and absolute truthfulness with oneself.

Rabbi Uri of Strelisk (d. 1826) was opposed to wonder-workers and sought ethical perfection from his followers.

Rabbi Yehuda Zvi of Rodzol (d. 1847) was the nephew of Rabbi Zvi Hirsch of Zhidikov.

Rabbi Yitzchak Meir of Ger (1789-1866) was a student of Rabbi Menachem Mendel of Kotsk and succeeded his master as leader of the dynasty. While maintaining the Kotsk devotion to truth, Rabbi Yitzchak Meir involved himself more actively with the day-to-day lives and troubles of the people.

Rabbi Zvi Hirsch of Zhidikov (1785-1831) was a student of Rabbi Moshe Lev of Sasov. His unique approach to Hasidism focused on strengthening the mystical foundations of the movement.

INDEX

INDEX OF LESSONS

Chapter 4: Measuring Performance

Chapter 5: Developing People

Chapter 6: Managing the Outside World

About The Author

Moshe Kranc has worked in high-tech for over 25 years, with 15 years in management positions in both the United States and Israel. Most recently, Moshe has served as Vice President of Research and Development for Jerusalem Venture Partners Studio.

Moshe was part of the Emmy-award-winning team that designed the scrambling system for DIRECTV and holds 5 patents in areas related to pay television and computer security. He lectures at the Jerusalem College of Technology, has published numerous technical articles, and was a member of The Association For Computing Machinery's Committee on Scientific Freedom and Human Rights.

Storytelling is part of Moshe's heritage – family tradition has it that he is descended from Rabbi Jacob Kranc, the Magid of Dubno, an 18th century itinerant preacher known as "the Jewish Aesop." For many years, Moshe has enjoyed collecting, reading and re-telling Hasidic stories to family, friends and colleagues. He has a unique perspective on the juncture of high-tech management and Hasidic tales, and the imagination to believe that they have something in common.

Moshe received his B.A. degree in Computer Science and Jewish Studies from Brandeis University, his M.Sc. in Computer Science from the University of California at Berkeley, and his M.Sc. in Management from Boston University.

Moshe lives in Jerusalem with his wife Elise and their children Aaron, Hannan, Tehilla, Jacob, David and Noam.